America's Role in Asia

Books By

D. F. Fleming

The Treaty Veto of the American Senate
(1930 and 1968)

The United States and the League of Nations, 1918–1920
(1932 and 1968)

The United States and World Organization, 1920–1933
(1938 and 1968)

Can We Win the Peace?
(1943)

While America Slept
(1944)

The United States and the World Court, 1920–1966
(1945 and 1968)

The Cold War and Its Origins, 1917–1960
(1961 and 1968)

The Origins and Legacies of World War I
(1968)

AMERICA'S
ROLE
IN ASIA

D. F. Fleming

Emeritus Professor of International Relations

VANDERBILT UNIVERSITY

Funk & Wagnalls

NEW YORK

To
The nearly five hundred thousand Americans
killed or wounded
And the five million Asiatic casualties
in the Korean and Vietnamese Wars

Contents

of reaction everywhere. 3. Oppose our anti-Communist obsession with facts. 4. Promote business partnerships with Communist countries. 5. Work constantly for détente with the Communist Powers. 6. Insist on domestic priorities. 7. Work to reduce our military and space budgets. 8. Encourage genuine business partnerships with the weaker peoples. 9. Give genuine, untramelled aid to the underdeveloped peoples through the United Nations and the World Bank. 10. Accept a fair revision of the terms of trade between the LDCs and the MDCs. 11. Really use the United Nations to grapple with the world's crucial problems. 12. Make our own democracy work. 13. Reorganize our national life and objectives for the long pull.

Preface

During the years 1965–1968 the American people suffered the greatest trauma of their national life, excepting
perhaps the period of the Civil War.

That conflict was tragic enough, in bringing death and
devastation to a large part of the country, yet great issues
were clearly involved. In Vietnam almost everything was
alleged to be at stake, yet belief mounted steadily that
nothing vital was. A large part of our youth rebelled at
being drafted for Vietnam jungles and a decisive part of
the national conscience revolted. It was not able to wit-
ness, day after day for three years, the use of every kind
of American firepower on a small, poor nation far away—
killing, maiming or displacing several millions of people
—without deep revulsion, a feeling which extended
around the world.

At home, too, bitter division and the dangerous diver-
sion of funds, attention, and good will from grave social
needs, produced dangers of revolt, or of national decay
at the foundations of the nation.

The eternity of bombing in Vietnam which President Johnson began with such total confidence and authority early in 1965 appeared to have ceased finally late in 1968, after it had ended his political career, changed the political face of the world, and raised starkly the question whether our national life is to be fitful and short.

Like multitudes of my fellow citizens, I did what I could to grapple with the great disaster that came upon us during these three years. This small book is offered as a partial, contemporary record of what happened; as an effort to estimate what responsibilities we have in Asia; and as an attempt to envisage a viable role for the United States in the world.

As one who has been a constant, involved observer of our wars over the past fifty years, and who cannot help seeing the giant world problems arising around us, I urge the reader to form some definite judgments of his own about what the United States can and cannot do in the world and to make his views known, while there is still time—before some fatal blunder ends our national life, if not civilization itself.

Some citizens have much more influence than others, but it is incumbent on each of us to identify the problems and dangers and to do what we can to help find a middle ground role in the world—between self-defeating isolationism and self-destroying globalism—one that we can sustain and other peoples accept.

Aside from the looming issue of national longevity that is involved, we also have the crucial stake of maintaining our democracy here at home, for if our leaders can go around the world forcibly cracking down on social dissenters, they will end by suppressing them at home. Yet constant orderly reform is essential to maintaining our democracy. It is therefore in double jeopardy from the foreign adventures of our military-industrial complex, including police-minded officials in Washington.

Accordingly, the old maxim that eternal vigilance is the price of liberty was never more applicable.

My thanks are due to the editors of *The Western Political Quarterly*, *The Progressive*, *The Annals* of the American Academy of Political and Social Science, *The Minority of One*, and *The New World Review* for permission to reprint articles previously published in their pages—and always to my wife for constant assistance in so many ways.

D. F. Fleming
Palo Alto, California
December, 1968

America's Role in Asia

1

What Is Our
Role in
East Asia?*

1965

The Cold War is twenty years old and it is obviously
waning in its main theater. During World War II Roosevelt and Hull labored long to create a basis for making
and keeping the peace in cooperation with the Soviet
Union, the great ally which had borne the heavy brunt
of the fighting on land and suffered most from death and
destruction. However, when Roosevelt and Hull passed
from the scene in 1945 their successors abruptly reversed
their policies and opted for conflict with the Soviet
Union over East Europe, and for the containment and

---

* This chapter was first published in *The Western Political Quarterly*
in March 1965. Except the epilogue, it was written before President
Johnson began the bombing of North Vietnam and the escalation of
the war on February 7, 1965.

encirclement of both the Soviets and Communism throughout the world.

The same complete reversal of healing policies had happened twice before in our history, after the death of Lincoln and after the fall of Wilson. In 1918 the tragic results of the reversal were delayed, but they came inexorably. The stupidities and agonies and infinite wastes of World War I had convinced many millions of the best citizens the world over that a new start had to be made, a league of nations must be created that would get all the nations into one body and prevent any more suicidal balance-of-power wars between rival alliances. Never in all human history had an overpowering need been so clear and clamant, yet it was quickly denied in the United States Senate, where the opponents of Woodrow Wilson preferred to return to isolation and let the world drift as before. Our lead in refusing responsibility for the peace was followed by Britain and France in the crises of the League of Nations, and the world drifted into a far worse world war in 1939.

We do not know that our leadership in the League of Nations would have made the difference, but we do know that we did not try to make it succeed, except futilely on the fringes of the League during the Manchurian crisis in 1931-1932. In 1945 we dutifully created another league of nations and entered it, but we also plunged at once into two crusades—an old-fashioned balance-of-power fight with the Soviet Union and a crusade against Communism everywhere. In other words, we heavily overcompensated for the failure of isolationism

4

by coming close to assuming responsibility for everything everywhere in the world.

Our quick assumption of global responsibility was signaled by Churchill's iron curtain speech at Fulton, Missouri, in March 1946, in Truman's applauding presence, and by the proclamation a year later of the Truman Doctrine, forbidding the expansion of Communism anywhere and in effect forbidding all revolutions around the globe, since they might turn Communist.

The Truman Doctrine was the rashest and most sweeping commitment ever made by any government at any time. In it Mr. Truman followed his own inclinations, and those of the advisers to whom he listened, and at the same time sought to foil his Republican critics, who had won the congressional elections of 1946 on charges of softness on Communism. No man ever gave greater hostages to fortune. Within two years the success of the Communist-led revolution in China punched a hole in Truman's Doctrine as big as a continent, one containing the world's largest and oldest people. A year later, in 1950, the Korean War broke out and President Truman was compelled to defend his global policy in what became a long, frustrating war. His Republican opponents at first applauded, but in the end they saddled him with "Truman's War," and it was primarily responsible for the defeat of his party in the 1952 election. Eisenhower went to Korea, as he had promised, and afterward accepted a stalemate peace.

Then for some seven years under the leadership of John Foster Dulles our objective was "liberation" and the "rollback" of both Communism and Russia in Europe. The Soviets did accept a negotiated withdrawal from Austria and they withdrew voluntarily from Finland, but the main lines of their World War II advance held. This was not strange, after what happened at Munich in 1938.

During the long years of the Cold War we were taught that there was a great Red Monolith which controlled all Communists everywhere, including the Chinese. Today, everybody knows that there is the deepest kind of split between Russia and China and that all the Communist states of East Europe are evolving lives of their own, usually in the direction of somewhat more freedom at home and better relations with the West. [This evolution, accelerating rapidly in Czechoslovakia, was rudely halted but apparently not ended by Soviet occupation of that country on August 20, 1968.] After leading the world in spending at least a trillion dollars on cold war armaments we have not been able to reverse the main result of World War II in Europe. There has been no rollback and we have come to understand that the terribly exhausted and devastated Soviet Union of the postwar years was both incapable of attempting and unwilling to attempt the world conquest which our post-Roosevelt leaders so hastily ascribed to her, and which we soon accepted as our first article of national faith.

In his last months President Kennedy gave us magnificent leadership in the direction of ending the Cold War. In his address at American University, on June 11, 1963, he acknowledged Russia's abysmal postwar weakness and called for a reappraisal of our attitudes toward her and toward the Cold War. President Johnson furthered this trend.

But there remains the Far East. There, Communist China has weathered severe setbacks and is gathering strength. She is also still in the militant stage of her revolution and very angry at us because of our support of the Chiang Kai-shek regime on Formosa and in the mouths of two Chinese harbors, because of our tremendous military power on Okinawa and along her coasts, and because of our other blockades of every kind—economic, diplomatic, and political. Moreover, she sees us occupying and fortifying the tips of two peninsulas on the Asiatic mainland, Korea and Vietnam, which are very close to her heartland. All the conditions for deep and permanent resentment on China's part are present.

For our part the prosecution of the Cold War in Asia has always aroused the strongest emotions of our political right wing. The defection of China to Communism had not been expected and it has never been forgiven. Nor has a much wider section of our people been able to forget the bitter frustrations of the Korean War. So why not simply turn the focus of the Cold War toward the Far East and keep our tremendous arms expenditures going another decade or two? And why not really push the Cold War to "victory" in Asia?

Before we go in this direction we should soberly review our involvements in Asia and try to ascertain what our objectives there are.

Korea

Korea is a good place to begin.[1] What does the record show there? It shows, first, that at the end of World War II we proposed the division of Korea at the 38th Parallel to prevent the Russians from occupying all of that country, which they could easily have done, and that they readily agreed. When our occupation forces finally arrived in Korea, on September 8, 1945, General Hodge found a Peoples Republic Government already organized by a national assembly representing all Korea. He suppressed this broadly representative government in the South and in the North the Russians managed to install their kind of rule. In the South we set up a rightist tyranny under Syngman Rhee, which was soon decisively repudiated in the election of May 30, 1950.

Contrary to the almost universal assumption, we do not know which side began the shooting in Korea on June 25. We do know that the North Koreans were well armed and ready and that they had been conducting a propaganda campaign for unification, but Rhee's government had been publicly threatening for months to march north. It had been defeated at the polls and may have been desperate. We do not know, either, that the Soviet government was behind the swift North Korean invasion of the South. It was boycotting the United Nations Security

[1] D. F. Fleming, The Cold War and Its Origins, 1917–1960 (Garden City, N. Y.: Doubleday & Company, Inc., 1961), II, 389–661.

Council at the time, in support of seating Red China in the United Nations, and was not present to veto United Nations' action in South Korea's defense. If Moscow knew about the invasion, would it commit such an obvious blunder?

We know that the United Nations quickly approved the Truman Administration's almost instant decision to fight to defend South Korea, and that on October 7, 1950, it very reluctantly approved our new objective of going north to destroy the North Korean government and unify Korea by force, the same thing which the North Koreans had attempted. This decision, as I see it, was the greatest single foreign policy mistake in our history. It converted a small war, already won, into a dreadful catastrophe which devastated Korea from end to end, killed some two million people and wounded another three million. By the time the war ended, South Korean military casualties alone had risen to 1,312,836 and the other side suffered a still greater slaughter.[2] Indeed, in the latter stages of the war our Army frankly labeled its objective to be "Operation Killer." The Korean War also cost us 144,173 American casualties and led us into the huge armaments budgets which still continue.

Is this the kind of "solution" toward which we are sliding gradually in South Vietnam? Before we answer "Yes, we must win," we should reflect on the results in Korea. There, after more than ten years, Rhee's oppressive government was finally overthrown by national student uprisings, to be succeeded by a veiled military

[2] *Encyclopedia Americana*, p. 387; *Time*, November 13, 1950, p. 23.

dictatorship. In South Korea we maintain an army of six hundred thousand Koreans, the fourth largest army in the world, most of whom would otherwise be unemployed or underemployed. Yet we also keep there on the front line fifty-two thousand American combat troops which cost us more than $100 million a year. This is a part of the approximately $3 billion annually which our world-wide military forces cost us—about the same as our annual balance-of-payments deficit, which we have had steadily since the Korean War build-up in 1950. Because of these ever mounting foreign deficits we now owe $25 billion in short-term indebtedness abroad and have only $4 billion in unearmarked gold to cover it. Senator Frank Church of Idaho has asked recently if this is to go on forever, in a discussion of "The Korean Paralysis." [3] What would happen if there should be bad economic weather in the world and worldwide loss of confidence in the dollar?

South Korea's Plight

What, too, is to be done about South Korea? Her agricultural economy is too weak to support her thirty millions, rapidly increasing, while in North Korea there are minerals, water power, and industries enough to make all Korea viable. The South Koreans know this and nothing can suppress a deep and growing yearning for the reunification of Korea, which would enable all to live in at least relative decency. We are apparently trying to

[3] *The Nation,* April 16, 1964, pp. 347–348.

turn South Korea back to Japan economically, but the South Koreans bitterly resent that kind of solution.

A dispatch from Seoul to *The New York Times* on May 31, 1964, states that discontent is running high, along with rapid inflation, that we had to send more than a million tons of food last year, that "20 per cent of South Korea's work force is unemployed and other heavy proportions are underemployed." But for the moment martial law, declared after conference with our officials in South Korea, represses student riots and demonstrations.[4] (Chapter 7 discusses later developments.)

Vietnam

As unrest simmers in South Korea what is the situation in Vietnam, another Asiatic peninsula?[5] There, during World War II, we at first aided the Communist-led revolution of Ho Chi Minh against the Japanese and the French. But later, as soon as the Communist nature of the revolution became evident, we took the side of the French in their effort to reimpose their colonial rule on the Vietnamese. Then our government increasingly poured every kind of aid into the hands of the French, deluging them with weapons and aid to the value of some $3 billion, but they could not win. With infinitely less aid from China the Vietnamese bled the French Army

[4] *Arizona Daily Star*, June 4, 1964 (*New York Times* Service).
[5] Fleming, *op. cit.*, pp. 667–706.

until by 1954 the French people could stand no more. Secretary of State Dulles fought hard to prevent the making of peace. He and Admiral Radford had plans for entering the war ourselves, but the reluctance of Congress and President Eisenhower prevented that and all of Mr. Dulles' threats could not avert the calling of a peace conference at Geneva. However, Mr. Dulles' stance of "angry negation" did prevent the victorious Vietminh from taking control of all of their country. Vietnam was divided at the 17th Parallel, temporarily, for two years only, to separate and demobilize the fighting forces, and became another tragic victim of the Cold War.

After eight years of French defeat the United States moved into South Vietnam in 1954 and set up another despot, Ngo Dinh Diem, who with Dulles' backing refused to permit the elections which the Geneva conference had called for in 1956 to unify the country, because he knew the other side would win. Washington stood behind the misrule of Diem's family for nearly ten years, until this finally led to an army rebellion in 1964. We backed the Diem tyranny because the Communists had renewed guerrilla war soon after the elections were frustrated, as they were expected to do. Lieutenant General S. T. Williams, chief United States military adviser in South Vietnam at the time, wrote in *U.S. News and World Report* on November 9, 1964, that he was instructed to expect attack from the North when the deadline for the elections expired in July 1956 without their being held.

This new war is now more than six years old and it is

reaching the proportions of the earlier one. Again we have poured in billions in weapons and supplies, and we have sent some twenty-two thousand American officers and troops to train the city boys of Saigon and other towns to go out into the jungles and fight their rural brothers, which they are not keen about doing.[6] We tell ourselves that the Viet Cong rebels are from North Vietnam—and some of them are, but relatively few.

The facts about who the rebels are have been stated in an authoritative book by Professor Robert Scigliano of Michigan State University. This university worked in South Vietnam under a large United States contract until the operation fell under Diem's disfavor. It is Scigliano's judgment that only "a small part" of the Viet Cong come from North Vietnam and that "nearly all of these have been Southerners who withdrew to the North after the Geneva agreements." The claim of massive infiltration from the North, he says, "does not appear to be supported by the available evidence." [7] This was verified in *The New York Times* as recently as July 5, 1964. In

---

[6] The extreme difficulty of inducing our protégés to become victorious fighters has been described many times in the dispatches, but never more clearly than in one from Malcolm W. Browne to *The New York Times* (and *Portland Oregonian*) on July 23, 1964. Referring to the apparently incurable habit of our trainees of getting themselves massacred in ambushes, a "high American officer" said: "We're begging, we're pleading, we're reminding them [the Vietnamese troops], we're cajoling: we cry, we stamp out in fury, we do everything, we bring them ice cream. But we haven't succeeded." What more could we do to make ferocious fighters out of people who don't have their hearts in it?

[7] Robert Scigliano, *South Vietnam, Nation Under Stress* (Boston: Houghton Mifflin Company, 1963), p. 148.

other words, even the Viet Cong from the North are patriots fighting in the land of their birth, and this is true even if they were born and trained in North Vietnam. [This remained substantially true also after our massive escalation of the war in February 1965, brought in large forces from North Vietnam.]

For many years our correspondents on the spot have testified that the Viet Cong were arming themselves by taking American weapons from our side. This has not been too difficult, since there is a false relationship between our officers and the conscripted youth of the towns, often seized forcibly. When two companies in an ambush broke and ran, "We beat them back to their positions with rifle butts, but finally there was no holding them," said U.S. Captain Ralph C. Thomas. He added that this was the second time in ten months that one battalion had fallen into ambush by violating the most elementary rules, and that some Vietnamese officers refuse to discuss battle plans in advance or even to consider American advice when it is offered. To most of them "the Americans' chief function is to provide equipment, supplies and air cover." [8]

 It should have been evident to us from the start that we cannot go into a far country and teach the youth to fight a deadly war against their brothers for our reasons. Failure was surely indicated by the ability of the North Vietnamese and Chinese to filter arms into South Vietnam, on the backs of men and in small boats at night,

[8] AP dispatch from Tra On, Vietnam, by John T. Wheeler, the *Arizona Daily Star*, December 20, 1964.

as they have been doing steadily in recent months. These supplies are rivulets, when compared to the mighty flood of war machines of every kind which we pour into South Vietnam, but they are sufficient to tighten steadily the Viet Cong ring around Saigon.

In its environs one of our supply ships has been sunk in port, a major airport has been shelled devastatingly and a hotel full of our officers bombed with grievous results. No American is safe, and a returning ship's officer reports that few Vietnamese shops will sell him anything lest they be bombed by the Viet Cong.

These rebels have the most vital things that men can fight for at stake, and it does not make them less determined to win when we destroy their villages and families with high explosives and napalm and defoliate their countryside with chemicals. We must not think that in using these methods we are killing Viet Cong alone, for much larger numbers of villagers also die. A dispatch of March 22 from Saigon to the *Arizona Daily Star* says: "The spectacle of children lying half alive with napalm burns across their bodies was revolting to both Vietnamese and Americans who entered the village."

This is one reason why the Viet Cong are winning the war: they control and govern some two-thirds of South Vietnam and there is small reason to believe that there will be time to put into effect the plans which we have for mastering the country and making it into a showcase of contented living. The South Vietnamese have been fighting for nearly twenty years, first against French rule, then against American control, and they are desperately tired of the never-ending strife. They may turn neutralist at any time.

In these circumstances we hear increasingly demands and plans [in late 1964] for bombing North Vietnam, to stop all aid from the North. [The bombing began early in 1965 and continued for more than three years.] It is wholly righteous for us to pour mountainous aid, including many troops, into South Vietnam, but diabolically wicked for trickles of aid to come in from North Vietnam. The advocates of victory at any price see these supply routes destroyed first, then the cities of North Vietnam, if necessary, and finally those of China, if the Chinese intervene, as they have already promised to do if we attack North Vietnam. They made the same pledge when we invaded North Korea in 1950. It is questioned now that the Soviets would honor their alliance obligations to defend China against us, yet Walter Lippmann warned us, on July 3, that "we must avoid the extreme of wishful thinking, which is to believe that in a war between China and the United States the Soviet Union would be neutral or on our side." We should remember, too, that on February 25, 1964, the Soviet Union warned the United States that if we extend the war into North Vietnam the Soviet people would render "the necessary assistance and support" to "the national liberation struggle in South Vietnam." [9] We might recall thoughtfully also that *years of bombing everything in sight in Korea did not give us victory there.* There, too, we had total control of the air.

[9] *The New York Times,* February 26, 1964.

It is quite true that China is in poor shape to fight and it is equally true that from our bases off her shores we have the power to turn China into a vast, helpless morass, or a desert, with our conventional and atomic bombs. The targets are all pinpointed, ready for the death of unlimited millions of Chinese. Even if it be granted that a nuclear world war could be avoided, we have the power to work our will upon China. Yet it does not follow that the Chinese leaders would fail to go to the aid of North Vietnam if we attack her. They believe deeply in the kind of war which won them control of China and which is winning in South Vietnam. There is also strong reason to believe that they think we would not risk the world-wide consequences of destroying their country with our super-weapons.

Consider the alternative to making peace which faces us. On August 3, 1964, the reliable Australian correspondent Denis Warner described the continued administrative and military decline in South Vietnam; the relentless rise of the Viet Cong forces to some two hundred fifty thousand, including battle-tested reserves; and Ho Chi Minh's ability to send his fifteen divisions throughout Southeast Asia, followed by "the Chinese divisions that lie behind." Saying flatly that victory for the South Vietnam government is out, Warner could find no military counter within our capacity except nuclear war. In other words, we would have to destroy Vietnam, at the least, perhaps most of Southeast Asia and presumably China, to "win." "The war," he said, "would have to be nuclear or it would be lost."

Why Are We in Vietnam?

Before we slide gradually into such a human and moral catastrophe we ought to ask ourselves very carefully what it is that we are fighting for in South Vietnam. For "freedom," it is commonly said. That is a word that comes easily to the tongue and there is no doubt that the Asiatic Communists do live under many regimentations and controls. On the other hand, there is small reason to believe that we could win a fair election in South Vietnam and no reason to believe that we could win an election covering the entire country. Among other reasons, the Vietnamese know that degrading poverty and destitution have been eliminated in China, and the liberty to eat is an elemental one. They would vote also for freedom from war and foreign control.

In the Eisenhower years it used to be said that we must not lose the tungsten mines and rubber plantations of South Vietnam. The latter are still mainly in French hands, and the French want the war stopped to save their investments. They still have half a billion dollars to lose. There is also much surplus rice in South Vietnam, of which we too have a surplus. But in the last analysis our reason for being in South Vietnam, beyond economic motives, is a belief that this peninsula is an extremely strategic spot and that if it "went" Communist, all Southeast Asia and beyond would turn Red.

This is the domino theory which has been used to justify every move in the Cold War. In 1947 it was said that if Greece went Communist so would Turkey, the

Middle East, Iran and beyond. So, too, would Italy and France in the West. In 1950 the Korean War was justified in the same way. We have been taught likewise that if Formosa were lost the Chinese would soon take the Philippines, then Hawaii, then Catalina Island and our own Pacific coast.

Under this theory any American intervention anywhere in the world can be justified. If South Vietnam "goes," it is said, then a long set of standing dominoes will fall down through New Zealand to the South Polar continent, which fortunately has been neutralized. But would they? The Vietnamese are a tough and patriotic people. They were ruled by China for centuries and have no wish to be again. Nor is there any evidence that Red China has dominated North Vietnam or North Korea. On the contrary, she has helped them both to industrialize, from her own limited means. China hopes to cut a big figure politically throughout the vast underdeveloped southern hemisphere. Would she begin by making colonies out of her small neighbors? North Vietnam and China do need the surplus rice of South Vietnam, but would they take it without payment?

Of course it is unthinkable to us that South Korea or South Vietnam should become Communist, but is that automatically involved in peace settlements which would neutralize both states by international agreements between the great powers, including China?

It would be a great gain to establish peace between the divided halves of Vietnam and Korea and permit them to trade with each other. There could be many slow stages in the drawing together of the North and South states. Neither would, or should, give up its presently established life quickly or without compromises and guarantees. I venture the belief that *we cannot prevent the reunion of these divided peoples indefinitely*, but that we can decide whether it is to be done gradually and by agreement, by revolution, or by war.

War With China?

Peaceful agreements would of course involve moderating our hostility to China, but is that really impossible? I well remember how we used to love the Chinese, when they were ragged, docile heathens, the subjects of our devoted missionary efforts. But since they became fighting men and Reds I note that they have become totally wicked. However, I observe also that we have been able to start ending the Cold War with the equally wicked Russians after they gained missile power capable of destroying us.

This, too, will happen in China in the next ten or twenty years, after which there will be no question of our clinging to the fringes of China and occupying islands in the Formosa Strait which she believes to be hers. [In early 1969, the growth of China's nuclear power was well ahead of expectations.] *When China gains the power to destroy us she will take control of the fringe of East Asia and leave it to us to convert a local war into a world holocaust.* The basic choice before us is between destroying China with our nation-killing weapons soon or beginning to make peace with her, as the other nations of the world are doing. We must choose the latter course if we are to remain a civilized people, and we could begin by permitting China to take the seat in the United Nations which is guaranteed to her by its Charter, before the other members seat her anyway. Then we could work for the neutralization and real self-government of the people of Formosa, while that is still a possible solution.

It is unreasonable to suppose that we can much longer control the entire Pacific Ocean, including the edges of Asia, against the will of the great powers and vast populations which live there. As in Europe, we shall have to accept the fact that World War II did have great and irreversible consequences in Asia. Max Freedman wrote from London on May 28 that "it is difficult for any British official to feel that Washington can have any enduring influence over the affairs of Laos and Vietnam, except at a price in men and money which the American people will refuse to pay." [10] On May 17 James Reston wrote that the French had learned three things: that however much the Vietnamese might differ from the Chinese they hated them less than the white man; that they are tough soldiers; and that no Western power could be established against China's borders.[11]

We are now learning the same things the same hard

[10] *Arizona Daily Star*, May 28, 1964.
[11] *The New York Times*, May 17, 1964.

way, but fortunately we do have leaders who recognize the inevitable. With his usual courage and candor, Senator Wayne Morse was the first high official to challenge the futility of our adventure in South Vietnam. He pointed out that we have always considered Southeast Asia to be beyond our defense perimeter and demanded an end to our Vietnamese adventure. On March 10, 1964, Senator Ernest Gruening of Alaska made the same demand. He asked that we stop wasting billions of dollars "seeking vainly in this remote jungle to shore up self-serving corrupt dynasts or their self-imposed successors." He considered every additional life sacrificed in this forlorn adventure a tragedy. He did not say, either, every "American" life. On February 19, 1964, Senator Mike Mansfield, the majority leader in the Senate, made a deeply impressive address in which he denied that any American national interest justified our assumption of primary responsibility in the Vietnamese war. "We have," he said, "teetered too long on the brink of turning the war in Vietnam, which is still a Vietnamese war, into an American war to be paid for primarily with American lives." [12] He was strongly supported by Senator E. L. Bartlett of Alaska, who deplored the way in which our policy in Southeast Asia was "locked in rigid, inflexible terms." He urged greater support of President de Gaulle's diplomacy, which calls for neutralizing Vietnam, and a less emotional and less abusive discussion of Communist China.

On March 25, 1964, Senator Fulbright, chairman of

[12] *The New York Times*, February 20, 1964.

22

the Foreign Relations Committee, made his historic address on thinking unthinkable thoughts. He did not ask for our withdrawal from Vietnam, but he did condemn the "relegating of an increasing number of ideas and viewpoints to a growing category of 'unthinkable thoughts.'" He noted that when we refuse to believe something because it displeases or frightens us, "then the gap between fact and perception becomes a chasm and actions become irrelevant and irrational." He urged us to think "about the festering war in Vietnam."

On the following July 10 a statement signed by five thousand university professors was issued in Washington calling for the neutralization of North and South Vietnam.[13]

It was doubtless impossible for the Johnson Administration to move in the direction of making peace in Southeast Asia and with China until after the 1964 political campaign was over. Now it will fail to do so at its peril. A Louis Harris opinion poll has already shown that more people favored neutralizing South Vietnam than opposed it, and that 45 per cent opposed expanding the war to North Vietnam and only 26 per cent favored escalation.[14] President Johnson must know, also, that the Republicans won the 1952 election on the frustrations of the Korean War and that they could win in 1968 on the frustrations of another endless war to regulate affairs on China's borders. Surely the President is astute enough to avoid carrying the albatross onus of a "Johnson's

---

[13] Portland *Oregonian*, July 11, 1964.
[14] *Washington Post*, March 30, 1964.

War." On the other hand, he can carry the country with him if he exerts strong leadership in making peace in Asia. The current Republican demand [in 1964] for victory and liberty in every part of the world is nothing less than a demand for American domination of the earth, but it is far too late for that. We have learned the limits of our power in Europe, and the limitations of our sway in Asia must also be learned. This will be very painful, since, as George Kennan said recently, the American tendency is "to view any war in which we might be involved not as a means of achieving limited objectives . . . but as a struggle to the death between total virtue and total evil." [15]

Our greatest investment in Vietnam is in prestige, but is our prestige to be conserved by making a bad matter steadily worse? It cannot truthfully be denied that the results of our efforts in Korea and Vietnam have been in both cases: division and tyranny, war and desolation, poverty and unhappiness for these small peoples. We have also achieved almost exactly the same results in Laos. Is this the way to conserve the prestige of the leader of the "free world"? And is wise and courageous action on our part to end such evils incapable of generating prestige?

[15] *The New York Times*, July 1, 1964.

24

The Urgency of Negotiation

The first essential is to recognize that our gamble in Vietnam has failed. In the six months since this article was first written the situation has gone from bad to much worse, both militarily and politically. Coup has succeeded coup and the military defeats have grown in magnitude. We tried hard to prove that we could learn anti-guerrilla war, for application on all continents, and we have failed. We could not succeed as alien mentors against the will of the Vietnamese people. Now there are almost no moral resources left in South Vietnam for continuing the war. Twenty years of it are more than enough.

Yet, astoundingly, there are people in Washington who now propound the doctrine of going on with "the manageable mess." *Newsweek* reported this development on January 11, 1965, quoting a specialist as saying: "It may take ten years or more of no-win and no-lose. . . . But with the resources at hand we can control this thing and bring it to a satisfactory conclusion."

This assumption that the long deterioration in South Vietnam can somehow be held in suspension defies all of the forces which are operating there. As one commentator on the 1964 CBS Annual World Affairs Roundup said about Diem's ten years as our man in Saigon, these were "wasted years. We supported an image, an illusion." Shall we now waste another decade in trying to support a kaleidoscope of unpopular rulers?

This is a self-defeating endeavor. As W. M. Bagby

observed in *The New York Times* on December 5, "The more overt our intervention, the more Saigon appears to be our puppet." We cannot successfully support dictatorships "propped up by feudal lords and white men," and "China cannot be kept out of Southeast Asia by white men." If our basic purpose is to keep her out, we would defeat it by extending the war and bringing in Chinese troops. Only a negotiated settlement can really forestall the entry of Chinese troops, first into North Vietnam and then in the South—an eventuality that all Vietnamese dread.

Inevitably, too, by our very presence in Vietnam we are dealing with China. We are not dealing simply with the three million people in the corrupt city of Saigon, but with some forty million Vietnamese, with about three-quarters of a billion Chinese, and with the Korean people. Each of these three nations is determined to have unity and freedom from foreign control, including ours.

Objections to Negotiation

But, it is said, our whole Asian policy would crumble if we turned toward negotiations with Peking. The reply is, said Emmet Hughes in *Newsweek*, January 11, 1965: "We do not seriously possess an Asian policy. Since World War II we have simply rushed—or stumbled—toward various ramparts." He might have added that this is the very essence of the Truman Doctrine, which launched us upon our anti-revolutionary career.

To the objection that we cannot negotiate from weakness, Hughes replies that the truth is that "one only negotiates from a position of weakness." Victors impose terms. He denies also that we have no negotiable assets to employ. We could offer to reduce our forces in Korea sharply, without eliminating a trip wire there, and China greatly needs trade with us.

This is one of those rare moments when level-headed men in the Congress and among our citizens can exert themselves effectively to turn their country from a bankrupt course into one that would bring both honor and profit to us. Time, too, is short. General de Gaulle is almost certainly right in believing that each succeeding month will see the growth of Communist strength in South Vietnam. We might remember also that it was the never-ending losses of French officers that signalized French defeat in Vietnam. Yet we have already committed enough of our "instructor" officers and noncoms to Vietnam to man four of our sixteen divisions, and we have already suffered one thousand eight hundred casualties.[16] Are we incapable of learning from the hard experience of others?

But the war-hawks cry in unison: "If we accept neutralization that will certainly be followed soon by a Communist takeover!" That could be. The long-run probability is that all of Korea and Vietnam may have to live through a period of evolving Communism, just as the East Europeans are. It is certain that peace in South Vietnam would mean strong participation in the government by the National Liberation Front, the political arm of the Viet Cong. But it does not follow that a coalition

[16] Bernard B. Fall, *The New Republic*, January 16, 1965.

27

government would fail. James Robinson, the Southeast Asia expert of NBC, said on December 29, 1964: "What we are fighting in Vietnam is an historical evolution. A neutrality there like Cambodia's is feasible. What we would have would be a coalition government that would last a long time."

Is this a worse prospect than deepening anarchy in South Vietnam and a complete Communist takeover? Peter Grose reported from Saigon in *The New York Times* on November 8, 1964, that the National Liberation Front (which is not entirely Communist) already has a shadow government which "covers all of South Vietnam," backed by powerful professional and guerrilla forces and "biding its time for a moment when leaders in Saigon turn in desperation to request a cease-fire." These parallel hierarchies, wrote C. L. Sulzberger on January 14, 1965, "have spread inexorably" as "Saigon's national administration has rotted. The fractional area it still holds is contested by rival warlords and political cliques." The "disaster hitherto nibbling at our heels now stares us in the face."

What is Feasible?

How much longer, too, can we continue to treat enormous China as something which does not exist, but which must be surrounded and "contained"? Surely this is an immaturity which we can no longer afford. We need to remember rapidly that the Chinese are not only the largest people in the world but by far the oldest in civilization, and perhaps the ablest. Certainly they have an unparalleled ability to survive. They are now united and strongly organized to advance into the twentieth century. It will be infinitely better for us to help them with trade than to fear and hate and fight them. Again it is left to West Coast leaders to see this. Governor Pat Brown of California recently said in Washington: "We have tried to get the world to join us in rejecting all economic and political ties with China." This policy "has failed, as the steady increase in trade with the Chinese Communists demonstrates. All we have left is the vigorous hostility of the Chinese which our policy has provoked." [17]

It is time we realized that such hatreds and such adventures as the Vietnamese war cannot be afforded. Twice in my lifetime the world has lived through the long agonies of world war. In 1914 the big governments blundered, stumbled and slid into war. Before 1939 three raging-tearing aggressor governments plunged the world into war—Hitler's Germany, Mussolini's Italy, and Tojo's Japan. Today we are having our very last chance to organize all of the governments and peoples—including the Chinese—into one group, the United Nations, for the purpose of establishing law and order and cooperation among them, in the atomic age. If we fail in this, Western civilization, at the least, will cease to exist. The choice before us is that simple and plain.

[17] *San Francisco Chronicle*, April 27, 1964.

We must therefore shake off the current dangerous delusion that strong-arm tactics can not only seize control of a great political party but get us anything we want in the world. We must work instead to establish a world community of all the peoples, while there is still time. "Let us," said President Kennedy more than a year ago, "make the most of this opportunity and every opportunity, to reduce tension, to slow down the perilous arms race, and to check the world's slide to final annihilation." [18]

This is certainly the only feasible course to take. It means giving up some of our aspirations for power on China's borders, some of our fixations that all Communist rule is wholly vile and that the law of social evolution never works in Communist countries. If power is what we must live by, we can still patrol most of the vast Pacific Ocean with our great sea and air armadas. We can still defend the Philippines from invasion, as we should, and perhaps Japan, though we cannot much longer prevent a large trade and closer relations between Japan and China. We can also help to stabilize the great Indonesia-Malaysia region.

A very impressive book by Robert G. Wesson has demonstrated with great cogency that our economic power base is declining rapidly, relative to the rest of the world. "Already," he warns, "the day is late." Since 1945 our power "to shape events has shrunk to less than half of what it was" and "the next fifteen years may well see

[18] D. F. Fleming, "The Turn Toward Peace," *The Annals*, January 1964, pp. 157–169.

America's potential in the world halved again." Instead of opposing the rise of other powers, he urges us to accept the reality of becoming "one of several equals" in a multipolar world. The United States, he cautions, "does not have leisurely time to become accustomed to a world changing to its detriment." His final admonition is that "the fixation of the cold war obscures vision, but reason can still play a part in making the best of an unpromising and worsening situation. With cool thought, much can be done to bring to pass that civilization means good, not evil." [19]

Certainly we will fail in the Pacific unless we look beyond power to friendly relations with China, to helping her to improve the life of her great people, as the Russians have already improved theirs, thus joining the ranks of the more contented and satisfied peoples. We have become good neighbors with the Japanese, whose Hiroshima ashes tell them that they can have no future war with China. The same ashes, which we do not like to remember, should tell us that we too must become good neighbors with China and that this is the best way to be truly helpful to her small neighbors, who could become prosperous if we removed from them the grievous burdens of arms, war and sundered nationhood.[20]

[19] Robert G. Wesson, *The American Problem: the Cold War in Perspective* (New York: Abelard-Schuman, 1963), pp. 6, 276, 280.
[20] On July 27, 1964, *Newsweek* (p. 41) published a careful estimate of China's readiness for war with us over Vietnam. It described modern new Chinese towns along the border; "about 300,000 troops in the area, with another 200,000 in reserve"; two full air force armies with 1,200 jet fighter planes nearby; and thousands of Vietnamese training in the hills.

Epilogue (written in 1965)

In the final stage of reading publisher's proof for this article, President Johnson ordered the bombing of North Vietnam, on February 7, 1965, after having won an overwhelming electoral victory over the fiery Goldwater in November as the safe candidate who would not go North, get into a big land war in Asia, or otherwise escalate the Vietnam War. However, he had thoughtfully provided himself with blank-check authority to make war in Southeast Asia during the Tonkin Gulf affair in mid-1964.

The bombing quickly followed humiliating losses in a guerrilla attack on our barracks and air field at Pleiku, but the main motive was to shore up our Saigon government from imminent collapse.

As this article is printed, the alternative is all too clear. No one could read the eight main articles and leading editorial in The New York Times *of February 14, 1965 without knowing that the United States had started on a collision course toward a nuclear world war, one which would kill one hundred million of us (Secretary of Defense McNamara's figure).*

If the Vietnamese war is escalated much further, no man may be able to stop it. Or, if catastrophe be avoided, we are headed toward a vast "limited" war throughout East Asia with the North Vietnamese, Chinese and

---

On July 18, Henry Tanner cabled from Moscow to *The New York Times* that Soviet officials have made it plain to foreigners on many occasions that the Kremlin could not hope to avoid being dragged into any full-scale war in Vietnam involving the United States.

North Korean armies, a war which could not be won. Nor would the responsibility be accepted or borne by the leading voices now crying for more and bigger bombings, including China's nuclear installations. If holocaust or exhaustion are to be avoided, President Johnson is entitled to strong and insistent backing by his true supporters for a policy of making peace in the Far East. The disaster alleged to be involved in political falling dominoes is minor and uncertain when compared to the imminent peril of the escalating military ones.

Our good name in the world is also at stake. We cannot compensate for losing the guerrilla war by imperiling everyone on earth. In the nuclear age there is no prestige in making war, or in trying to determine the internal affairs and civil wars of little nations everywhere. Nationalism is defeating all those who make this attempt, and it will continue to do so. There is prestige in leading for peace. In the terms of the Times editorial, this is a time to achieve greatness by restraint. It is also high time for a peace conference in which the United Nations plays the healing role for which Secretary General U Thant is so well fitted.

2

Can We
Play God
in Asia?*

1965

At this moment every American citizen is involved in
what is probably the most dangerous international confrontation in our entire national history. It is a new kind
of confrontation, one which could not even have been
imagined fifty years ago. It is a contest between the will
of a half-dozen men at the summit of our government—
with a greatly divided country watching fearfully—against
the will of a billion or more Asians caught up in a "revolution of rising expectations" and in a mighty determination to be rid of all forms of Western control.

Faced with frustration in their efforts to impose their
own solutions to the problems of the Vietnamese people,
the chief decision-makers in the United States have

* Reprinted from *The Progressive*, June 1965.

resolved, as the President asserted on April 7, 1965, that "We will not be defeated. We will not grow tired. We will not withdraw, either openly or under the cloak of a meaningless agreement."

Exactly two months earlier, on February 7, when the shelling of our barracks and planes at Pleiku signalized vividly how badly we were losing the guerrilla war in Vietnam, Mr. Johnson abruptly determined that the trouble lay in North Vietnam, that the North Vietnamese were "aggressors" who must be bombed from the air.

Is South Vietnam a State?

The justification for this new "wider war" rests entirely upon the disastrous fiction that the government of South Vietnam is an independent sovereign state with which the North Vietnamese have no legitimate concern, but with which we have every right to deal on our own terms. This position ignores a number of highly relevant factors.

In 1954, under the leadership of Ho Chi Minh, the Vietnamese people won their struggle for independence against the outdated and immoral attempt of France to reassert her rule over Vietnam, after having surrendered the country to Japan during World War II.

The 1954 Geneva Conference of nine governments, which ended the war, split the country into two zones in its efforts to stop the shooting, but never intended to divide Vietnam permanently. It stated, rather: "The conference recognizes that the essential purpose of the agreement on Vietnam . . . is to end hostilities. The military demarcation line is provisional and should not in any way be interpreted as constituting a political or territorial boundary." Elections designed to reunite the country were directed by the Conference, to be held by July 1956, under international supervision.

The elections were frustrated by President Ngo Dinh Diem, whom Secretary of State John Foster Dulles had selected to rule South Vietnam, because both knew that the vote would almost certainly be for union under a Communist-oriented leadership. The South Vietnamese government is, therefore, our own creation, and our now canonized "word" to defend it was given to the tyrant Diem, who was finally deposed and murdered and who has been succeeded by a kaleidoscopic array of unpopular and ineffective rulers.

Because we are not a signatory to the Geneva Treaty of 1954, and have violated its terms by injecting our arms and troops into South Vietnam, we have no legal standing in Vietnam, South or North. We are there only by unilateral action, by our own will, for our own purposes, ostensibly at the "invitation" of our client regime in Saigon, which would have ceased to exist years ago if dependent on its own mandate to rule. The South Vietnam government survives, however tenuously, only because of United States bayonets and bombs, and because of the continuing lavish expenditure of billions of dollars by the United States.

Our attacks upon North Vietnam contravene the most basic principles of international law. They clearly violate our United Nations obligations to "first of all seek solution by negotiation" and to report any alleged measures of self-defense "immediately" to the Security Council. We are also committed by the United Nations Charter to refrain "from the threat or use of force" against any state. Yet our actions in Vietnam portend for other nations that the United States is prepared to force its will by bombs and bullets whenever the Administration thinks its foreign policy aims are being frustrated.

The principal motive for our assertions of global mastery seems to be the belief that if revolution succeeds in Vietnam it will succeed in many other places. This is what Walter Lippmann, the celebrated columnist, called, on March 31, 1965, "the half-baked notion that the war in Southeast Asia will be decisive for the future of revolutionary unheavals in the world." It is sad indeed that Lippmann should have to remind us that "revolution is a home-grown product" and that it could not be stamped out, once and for all, "by stamping out Red China."

Are All Methods of Suppressing the Revolution Justifiable?

The scope of our actions in Vietnam discloses the enormity of this obsession which has seized our leaders. It sets a dangerous precedent for the United States to become both the judge of the "democratic" nature of any internal revolt, and the wielder of repressive force against any uprising of which we disapprove. Such a policy repudiates the principles of our Declaration of Independence, and denies the innate right of every people to revolt against intolerable conditions.

Our man Diem's rule in South Vietnam provoked a great rebellion. Edgar Snow has described unforgettably how Diem's agents "mopped up" hundreds of villages, arresting, plundering, torturing people, and often burning villages—on the theory that they must contain some enemies of Diem's regime. These outrages generated a country-wide guerrilla revolt, which began and still centers in the *southern* part of South Vietnam. It received little aid from North Vietnam until recent months. This aid, whether from Hanoi or Peking, has never been more than a trickle compared to the billions of dollars in military aid which the United States, a land across the world, has poured into Saigon's hands in an ever-rising flood. [In the years after this was written, both the Soviet Union and China gave North Vietnam enough aid to keep the war going.]

United States methods of suppressing the rebellion have served instead only to greatly exacerbate it. We have used helicopters carrying sharp-shooters, napalm in large amounts, bombers, needle shrapnel, defoliants that kill vegetation and crops, and noxious gas, and we have made attempts to burn whole forests, but the rebellion still gathers strength. Our efforts have generated hatred among the Vietnamese people and inspired bloody Viet

Cong reprisals against Americans in Saigon. Currently, unable to suppress the rebellion in the South, we are relentlessly bombing the "aggressor" state of North Vietnam, the half of the divided Vietnamese nation which is hungry and dependent on foreign aid because it is cut off from the rice of South Vietnam.

Will Hanoi "Get the Message"?

Those who wield our will in Washington seem assured that, as devastation spreads inexorably in North Vietnam, Hanoi will "get the message" and call off the Viet Cong in South Vietnam. But it is questionable that Hanoi could do so, even if it wished. It is far more likely that the large North Vietnamese army will finally leave its devastated country and move south to fight against us.

Beyond North Vietnam lies China. Might Washington not decide that Peking has committed the crime of aggression by persuading the North Vietnamese not to surrender? Will this be the route to a war on China? This may soon seem to Washington, according to the President's thinking, to be the only way to prevent the Administration's ultimate defeat in Southeast Asia and of its avowed policy that "we will not be defeated." On April 11, 1965, Undersecretary of State George W. Ball was quoted by the Associated Press as saying that the United States would carry out its "commitment" in Vietnam even if this meant war with China and the Soviet

Union. The President himself said ominously, on April 7, "Over this war—and all Asia—is another reality: the deepening shadow of Communist China. The rulers in Hanoi are urged on by Peking."

Mr. Johnson has "no desire to devastate that which the people of North Vietnam have built with pain and sacrifice," but he is fully and obviously prepared to do so, for he continued: "We will use our power with restraint and with all the wisdom that we can command. *But we will use it.*" (Emphasis added.)

The President is a humane man, but he seems to have said that he will use whatever amounts of the vast powers at his fingertips that he believes to be necessary to enforce his will in Asia. [Before leaving office in January, 1969, a victim of his "restrained" use of power, he had presided over the killing of several hundreds of thousands of poor Vietnamese, the maiming of larger numbers, the driving of some three-million to helpless squalor in the cities, and the devastation of their country by every known scientific means, except use of nuclear power. His bombing had broken World War II records, and he had sickened his own people and horrified the world.]

Shall We Bomb China Next?

It seems increasingly clear that the main target is China, the new source, for United States leaders, of all world evil. There is no blinking at the fact, either, that our only hope of avoiding ultimate defeat in Asia, if current United States thinking is to be carried to its logical conclusion, is to attempt to destroy China now— even if hundreds of millions die—before that nation has developed effective nuclear capability. Every target in China that seems to matter is already pinpointed from our plentiful launching points all along China's coasts.

Air Force Major General John P. Lavelle, in testimony presented in February 1965, before a House Appropriations subcommittee, stated that the United States has selected its targets in China and in the event of general war could "inflict an unacceptable level of destruction" on that nation with missiles. "Vastly detailed" studies are ready to "return China to the dark ages," if necessary, according to a report from Washington in *The Wall Street Journal*, March 5, 1965. The survey emphasizes that we would probably begin by bombing "along the enemy's supply lines all the way back to the home-front factories" and we "could plaster almost at will such targets as petroleum and ammunition dumps, air fields, rail hubs, and bridges . . . nuclear bombs would also be available if the President decided to use them."

Doubtless this terrible progression would proceed "with restraint and with all the wisdom we can command," but before the United States slides, by carefully planned stages, into this bottomless pit we should pause to reflect on the cataclysmic consequences of a war with China— not to mention the Soviet Union. The Chinese leaders and their deeply-indoctrinated people believe firmly that hundreds of millions of tough human beings can defeat any aggressor in China. Chou En-lai has already said, in Algiers on March 30, 1965, that China expects to be bombed by the United States but that she believes her many millions of trained people will win the war, however long it might take.

We should be prepared for the fierce anger of the Chinese that would increase with such bombings, if they should ever take place, and for the growing wrath of virtually all of Asia and most of the rest of the world. President Johnson's Baltimore speech on April 7, 1965, was forced by "public and private demands for negotiation from leading Democrats in Congress, from intellectuals, from an energetic letter-writing public at home, from his closest allies, from neutral nations, from the United Nations and from the Soviet Union," according to Max Frankel, writing in *The New York Times* the following day. What this means is that the relentless bombing of North Vietnam by United States forces had already stirred world opinion to an unprecedented unanimity of opposition to our government's policy in Asia.

Must We Rule the Entire Pacific World?

Before we turn all humanity against the United States we should weigh, with humility, these considerations: There is a manifest vanity in our assertion of control over the entire Pacific Ocean and the islands and fringes of China on the far side of it. This is clearly an untenable position. Southeast Asia may be a core interest of China; it is, after all, in her dooryard. But it is dubious that the United States, half a world away, shares an interest of comparable depth.

Our dominoes-of-disaster theory is a dangerous illusion which in reality works in reverse. Rather than the political dominoes falling away from us in all directions, presuming that we "lost" Southeast Asia, we are instead causing them to fall rapidly away from us now through our very effort to hold South Vietnam by every conceivable means, the prospect of world war included.

Even our closest allies reveal growing apprehension of our bomb-into-submission policy. Japan is increasingly restive. So are the Philippines, where feeling is rising against us not only on this but on other grounds. Indonesia is militantly opposed to United States policy in Asia. India, in spite of her border wars with China and Pakistan, is angry with us. Pakistan is friendly with China, and we must expect the mounting indignation of the Soviets to force Soviet intervention at some stage.

There is nothing in this defiance of world opinion that will win friends, or keep those few on this issue that we have left. Walter Lippmann spoke precisely on this when he wrote about our "drifting into icy isolation."

The people of Vietnam have a right to self-determination, and we have denied it to them ever since 1956, whether they choose to determine their future by "free elections" or by revolution. We should remember also that we ourselves once waged a revolution, and with infinitely less reason.

We cannot achieve peace while refusing to negotiate with the National Liberation Front in South Vietnam, which receives the loyalty of far more people there than does the nominal government of South Vietnam which we support. We refuse to deal with an organization of Vietnamese that represents a major portion of the populace, on the grounds that the NLF is Communist. Yet a high Japanese diplomat sent by his government to investigate the situation in South Vietnam returned to report, according to a *New York Times* account, that "even the people of Saigon" estimate the proportion of Communists in the Viet Cong to be "at most thirty per cent."

We cannot achieve peace by agreeing, as the President has done, to negotiate unconditionally with everybody except our real antagonist. This is a formula for avoiding negotiation. Professor Staughton Lynd, Yale historian, commented aptly, in a letter in *The New York Times* on April 14, 1965, that while we use "gas, torture, and napalm to crush an indigenous social revolution, a Mekong Delta Authority will be a fig leaf to hide barbarism."

We must reexamine our obsession that all Communism is intrinsically vile and that Communist societies never evolve into something better.

Cruelly divided peoples such as the Vietnamese and the Koreans have a right to unity and they will achieve it, if the holocaust of a world war is avoided. It should be our goal to help them attain unity, perhaps by stages, with as many guarantees of their independence and neutrality as we can obtain.

By attempting since 1950 to blockade, by every means, the new China, we have won the bitter hatred of the Chinese people, and this can be undone only slowly. But it must be undone, since our whole future depends on it. Enormous as is the obliterative power in the hands of our President, it is not sufficient to establish a *Pax Americana* over the entire earth.

Entirely aside from the moral issue, there is not even prestige to be gained by bombing other peoples into submission. After all, France lost an eight-year war of conquest in Vietnam in 1954. She was defeated in Algeria a few years later and made the best of it. Charles de Gaulle, the man who was installed in power to "save" Algeria for France, wisely eased France out of Algeria. He "lost" it and the loss was extremely painful and humiliating, but his prestige today is higher than ever. Doing what is right generates prestige; doing what is wrong destroys it. [Later, de Gaulle lost his prestige when he meddled in the affairs of Canada, barred Britain from the Common Market, stopped the Market's evolution toward political union, and sought to make himself the arbiter of Europe. Seeking power, he neglected badly needed internal reform and prepared the ground for troubled times and the loss of all the glory he sought.]

Where Will it End?

Today we are confronted by a deadly dangerous decision. If our nation's leaders insist on control of Southeast Asia they will have to send great numbers of United States forces to conquer it on the ground, and to police East Asia over a long period against the hatred of a billion Asians. That would be necessary to prevent the Chinese from *ever* becoming an atomic power again. Hanson Baldwin, military expert of *The New York Times*, suggests that a million troops may be required to effectuate our will in that area and he did not allow for a long occupation of Southeast Asia and China against never-ending guerrilla attack. This is the abyss before which we stand.

It is far too late for us to attempt to play the role of God in Asia, let alone on all the continents. As our bombers range farther and farther north in Southeast Asia, attempting to impose our leadership's will, the words of two thousand five hundred clergymen whose statement was published widely in the press on April 4, 1965, should ring ever-louder in the White House, the Pentagon, and the State Department—"IN THE NAME OF GOD, STOP IT!"

Our leaders are naive if they expect mature men and women to credit their offer of "unconditional discussions" while they bomb at will throughout Southeast Asia. This is a perfect method for *preventing* negotiations, for making them impossible. It is also, in effect, a demand for unconditional surrender.

President Johnson is advised by men who have been consistently wrong about Vietnam. Only a powerfully-expressed public opinion can rescue our leaders—and all of us—from their desperate gamble in Asia. For the first time in our entire national history we stand on the brink of moral self-annihilation, with the physical destruction of a large part of the world a constantly increasing possibility.

3

Can *Pax Americana* Succeed?*

1965

The constant thunder of our bombing attack on North Vietnam, twelve thousand miles away in Asia, raised insistently the question of our ability to police the earth and to suppress anywhere in the "free world" rebellion that was Communist led, or might be.

Did the United States have any moral mandate for such an endeavor? Were its resources of men, money and will sufficient? Would the end result be the final world war? Or if this could be avoided, would we find ourselves eventually walled in by an involuntary Fortress America with barriers of distrust, fear, hatred, and even armament arising against us?

* First published in *The Annals* of the American Academy of Political and Social Science, July 1965.

While the Vietnam tragedy was stirring Asia to its depths, a sudden United States intervention in Santo Domingo touched off waves of anger and apprehension against us throughout Latin America, and competent investigators found even Western Europe turning its back on us, partly because of our relentless takeovers of European businesses. Only action by our true conservatives could control Washington's *Pax Americana* outthrusts [a development which did occur some three years later, in the spring of 1968, as recorded in Chapter 8].

It is very difficult to realize the great change that has come over our prospects, both as individuals and as a nation, since February 7, 1965.

Up to that time we had every right to look forward to a far better future at home and abroad than we have had for decades. We had elected a president who has a deep and sincere desire to halt our vast expenditures for "defense"—swelling well toward the trillion-dollar mark since the Cold War began. He had actually reduced the defense budget a little—only a little, but a precious change of direction.

At last the great wildernesses of Cold War neglect in our home life were to be tackled—our starved schools and overcrowded colleges; our inadequate hospitals; the shameful jungles of our city slums; great areas of the hopeless rural poor; our dying commuter railroads and choked highways; our foul and dangerously polluted rivers and harbors; our choking and health-destroying city smogs; our neglected treatment of mental illness; our stubborn unemployment problem and the menace to so

49

many people's reason for being in rising automation; burgeoning crime syndicates apparently beyond the reach of law; personal assaults in public places making everyone unsafe but stirring no aid to the assaulted; and, not least, freedom and justice and dignity for our Negro citizens.

All these and many other evidences of a rundown society, too long absorbed in frustrating other peoples' purposes, were being tackled under the superb leadership of President Johnson, with his noble, down-to-earth vision of a Great Society. Yet suddenly, almost in a twinkling of the eye, all of our hopes for a better future were clouded by the President's abrupt decisions to seek solutions for revolutionary conditions in Asia and Latin America by the exercise of our vast military power. The arms budget is on the way up again, and now no man can count on peaceful progress.

Abroad, too, the other side of our outlook was equally bright. The grisly image of the alleged Red monolith had receded. Every intelligent citizen knew that social evolution was taking place very rapidly in the Soviet Union and throughout East Europe. President Johnson had declared, on December 18, 1963, that we want "to see the Cold War end; we want to see it end once and for all."

Moscow and Washington talked publicly about exchange visits of the heads of state; direct air service with the Soviet Union was about to be approved along with other openings of still-closed windows to understanding —even friendship. The long night of the Cold War

seemed about over. Its end had been signaled resoundingly by the overwhelming defeat of Senator Goldwater
in November, who had been rejected first and foremost
because we believed he would be trigger-happy and ruthless in the use of our immeasurable national power.

When the American people went to bed on the night
of February 7, they had every right to believe that these
immensely beneficial trends, both at home and abroad,
would lead on into a civilized and humane world in
which they and other peoples could breathe freely and
attack their problems confidently.

North Vietnam Attacked

But on that night something happened at Pleiku, in
South Vietnam. A band of ragged Viet Cong walked
into one of our barracks compounds, found all the guards
asleep, and blew up the barracks, with heavy American
casualties. Then they did the same thing to our planes
on a nearby airfield. Similar events had happened in
Vietnam before, without the earth being shaken to its
foundations, but this time President Johnson suddenly
yielded to advisers who had long been urging the bombing of North Vietnam and seized the occasion to attack
North Vietnam, in violation of all international law,
including the United Nations Charter.

This decision was made for two reasons: because our
attempt to suppress the Viet Cong rebellion had obvi-

ously failed and because "governmental instability in South Vietnam threatened to bring about a total collapse of the effort there." [1] The desperate decision was therefore made to attack North Vietnam, to stave off collapse in the South by encouraging our protégés there, and to try to close the comparative trickles of aid coming from the North to the Viet Cong.

The President ordered the bombing of North Vietnam to begin at once, selecting the targets himself, and it has continued since—more than three months as this is written in May 1965. During this time we have been told daily that the North Vietnamese are aggressors (in their own land) while we are only defending a sovereign nation in South Vietnam.

World War Or Local Victory?

This reasoning, enforced by perpetual bombing, leads straight on to the bombing of China. President Johnson has already spoken ominously of "the deepening shadow of China" and has alleged that "the rulers of Hanoi are urged on by Peking." The thunder of our bombs also drives China and Russia slowly toward each other, in spite of their deep antagonisms, and our new definition of "aggression" may even compel the bombing of the Soviet Union, precipitating the final world war.

It would be shortsighted indeed not to brace ourselves

[1] Tom Wicker, The New York Times, May 4, 1965.

for this to happen, but the President's often repeated promise to use our power "with wisdom and restraint" leaves open another possible outcome. Accepting negotiations with the Nine-Power Geneva group of 1954, including the Viet Cong National Liberation Front, would involve the neutralization and unification of North and South Vietnam. This appears to be ruled out by the President's adamant insistence on April 7 that we must have the independence of South Vietnam guaranteed and that: "We will not be defeated. We will not grow tired. We will not withdraw, either openly or under the cloak of a meaningless agreement."

This leaves as a way out only the relentless imposition of our will on Vietnam, North and South. It involves the destruction of every element of strength in both parts of the country which is susceptible to bombing and the sending of large numbers of American troops to dig the Viet Cong out of the jungles of South Vietnam.

It may be that the lack of enough nuclear arms in China would compel extreme forbearance on the part of the Communist powers while our mastery of Vietnam is made good. Since the Chinese may feel compelled to hold their hand, it is not too soon to consider the effects of our "victory" in Southeast Asia.

According to our hard-liners everything would then fall into place. Southeast Asia would be "saved." Everyone in the world would know who was top dog. We would be spared the intense humiliation of admitting that a guerrilla revolution can succeed and, with the contrary demonstrated in Vietnam, all other revolutions around the globe could be suppressed, by the same terrible measures if necessary but probably with less effort. We would not have to fear wars of liberation or the contraction of our free-enterprise living space thereafter.

Pax Americana

Inevitably, too, this image of the future grows in many minds in many lands, as the application of sheer power by us in Asia proceeds. Nor would it be wise for us to dismiss or discount too soon the deep currents in our life which run in the direction of a *Pax Americana*.

As early as February 17, 1941, Henry R. Luce spoke for powerful segments of conservative thinking when he called for "The American Century," asking us "to accept whole-heartedly our duty and opportunity as the most powerful and vital nation in the world and in consequence to exert upon the world the full impact of our influence, for such purposes as we see fit and by such means as we see fit."

This expression of imperial will did not have the support of President Roosevelt, but in 1945 his sudden death brought to power a president who quickly became committed to "containing" both the Soviet Union and Communism. As in Vietnam in 1965, there was in Greece after 1945 a Communist-led social revolution which apparently was supported by a majority of the people. Therefore, in March 1947, Mr. Truman issued his famous Doctrine which came very close to forbidding revolution anywhere in the world thereafter. The heart of the Truman Doctrine was the declaration "that it must be the policy of the United States to support free peoples who are resisting attempted subjugation by armed minorities or by outside pressure." Mr. Truman insisted on the word "must."

In these sweeping terms he meant to forbid any future revolutions that were Communist-led, or supported by outside Communists, but by outlawing revolt by armed minorities he proscribed all revolutions.

This, too, has been the heart of our policy to this day. It was the main motive for the Marshall Plan, which should have preceded the Doctrine, and—after one revolution did turn Communist, in Cuba—of the Alliance for Progress. This guiding fear of revolution that might be Communist helped to bring about the North Atlantic Treaty Organization (NATO), the Central Treaty Organization (CENTO), the Southeast Asia Treaty Organization (SEATO), and all the other segments of the great rings of containment.

But it was all very frustrating. For nearly twenty years containment sent us rushing from one brink of war to another, in an effort to put out fires that might extend Communist areas. The negativism of the policy steadily built up in our right wing an ever-mounting and angry frustration which finally took control of the Republican party at San Francisco in 1964 and nominated Barry Goldwater, a candidate dedicated to victory by power, everywhere.

He was defeated. In 1965, President Johnson refuses to be, but can his extremely powerful consensus pressures really bring along the liberal Democrats, who supplied his great majority, into a national policy of using our power everywhere that revolution, or conflict that might lead to revolution, arises?

The doctrinal basis for a *Pax Americana* policy is virtually complete. In his April 7, 1965, address the President disavowed any desire to "impose our will or to dictate" the institutions of others. But, he continued, "we will always oppose the effort of one nation to conquer another." In using the word "nation" he begged completely the question of the nature of the struggle in South Vietnam, and left the way wide open to intervene in every civil war and to decide any conflict between two states, since the threat of conquest can be defined as elastically as "nation" to shelter any regime that we may wish to preserve.

The intent to make his will prevail, first in Vietnam and then wherever he decides it is necessary, could not have been clearer. The Truman Doctrine had virtually forbidden any violent social change anywhere, and the Johnson Doctrine has now reaffirmed the prohibition in the sternest tones.

There remains the question of enforcement, and ample power is at hand. Any American president has at his fingertips the power to destroy civilization itself, at least in the North Temperate Zone, and he is now equipped with every conceivable gradation of military power, and with the most "sophisticated" theories and rules for applying it in "limited" wars. To be sure there is the ever-present danger of escalation getting out of hand, but this need not deter a self-confident president from taking many escalated steps to enforce our kind of order in the world.

Accordingly, it is essential to begin to think ahead to the probable results. The war-game players have been doing it for years, and they have now captured our citadel of power. It is high time that the rest of us try to foresee the course and consequence of firm applications of escalated power, since everything depends on the outcome.

To begin with, the Soviet Union and Eastern Europe are under the Russian nuclear umbrella, and perhaps China. Much depends on the power of rising anger in the Soviet people and their leaders while our subjugation of Vietnam proceeds. In any event, there is only one way to prevent China from taking control of her own coasts, harbors, and islands some time in the next decade or two: to destroy her atomic installations and much else now, and keep them from ever being rebuilt, either by periodic bombing or permanent occupation. This is the real price of imposing our will on Southeast Asia and China now. We must be prepared to practice genocide in China.

Asia Aroused Against Us

The largest, toughest, and perhaps the ablest people in the world will not otherwise submit to our close blockade, by every known means, including control of the two Asiatic peninsulas which guard her from both the North and South. Also in her struggle to assert herself in her own region, China is likely to have the warm support of some 750 million other Asians. In spite of her border wars with China, India is already very angry with us for our conduct in Vietnam, as are the Indonesians. Pakistan opposes our tactics. The Philippines are restless, and the Japanese people are increasingly critical and fearful of our policy.

It would be rash not to count soon on the united opposition of all Asians to our reassertion of white control on Asia's doorsteps. This is a jeopardy in which the British in Malaysia also stand with us. It does not require any sophisticated reasoning among the most illiterate Asiatics to tell them that yellow and brown backs are again bared to the white man's lash, this time administered horribly in several ways from the skies. This is why Senator Morse, one of the two most courageous men in the United States and one of the wisest, said at Stanford University that the Second World War had ended all forms of colonialism in Asia and that "the Asians will bury it." With their different "values in time, life and materiality," this is what we must expect. What appears to our leaders to be a righteous protection of freedom for our clients on the rim of Asia is bound to seem to the Asiatics the remnants of a bygone age which must be destroyed. It could cost them a hundred million lives, or more, to expel us from Asia, but there would be enough of them left.

In the process we could destroy much that is material in Asia while killing in ourselves all that is moral and spiritual. We can cling to a vast arc of containment around the rim of the new China only by measures that would put us beyond the pale of humanity. Is this a road we can afford to travel?

Europe Turns Against Us

While we are facing West with our inveterate faith in being able to master anything in that direction, the East is closing behind us in Europe, the very area which we had thought secured to us firmly by our great efforts and expenditures in containing the Soviet Union. This is a development of which most Americans are unaware, but consider the mounting evidence.

The turn of Europe away from us has been accelerated by the great outthrust of American investments from giant corporations with very great tax-released profits to invest. With the Americanization of Canada's economy well-advanced, to the extent of some $13 billion, prosperous Europe exerts an inevitable lure. "All across Western Europe a new, growing wave of resentment has been building up against American corporations which seek a foothold on the continent," wrote Bernard D. Nossiter in the *New Republic* on April 10, 1965. "Opposition to the American dollar as it pours into West Germany, capturing entire companies or taking over parts of other firms, has sharply increased," reported a *Los Angeles Times* writer from Bonn on February 14, 1965.

A careful European survey by Senior Editor Arnaud de Borchgrave of *Newsweek* on March 8, 1965, found our economic power to be practically irresistible—our economy growing at $40 billion a year; $20 billion spent by our companies yearly for research and development; $1 billion collected annually in patent fees from three Western European countries; General Motors with $5 billion in world sales, two hundred thousand different products, and $500 million to invest in European expansion; and our investments in West Europe up $10 billion to $11.5 billion in the past decade and expected to rise to $24 billion by 1975. Said a prominent German banker: "The rate at which the Americans have been gobbling up small European companies is positively indecent."

Other observers agreed that against the mighty outflow of American takeover dollars only one economic defense was possible, the rapid formation of giant European combines able to battle ours on Europe's home grounds. This logically required the quick formation of a United Europe politically, to assist and control the new corporate behemoths.

Faced by the essential question "to be or not to be," quick developments in Europe were to be expected. Nevertheless, the results of Arnaud de Borchgrave's second European tour two months later, reported on May 3, 1965, are sensational. He found nothing less than "a major regrouping of Western and Eastern European nations, including Britain, that could cut sharply into the remaining influence of the U.S. on the Continent."

The debate in Europe is no longer between "Atlanticists" and "Europeans," he continued. "The burning issue is how to end the artificial split between the French-led Common Market and the British-backed European Free Trade Association as a preparation for joining up with Eastern Europe, in a grand new order." The real debate is whether to stretch this new order to include Russia, as Zorin, Russia's top diplomat arrived in Paris as Ambassador to France and Soviet Foreign Minister Gromyko followed him to receive a royal welcome in Paris.

Even in Britain, de Borchgrave found pressures building to break out of the Atlantic mold, that is, close association with the United States. The British Tories had concluded, to quote one of their top leaders: "A home market of 50 million consumers is not enough. And it is no good looking toward the U.S. There is no room for Britain in the pattern of America's economy." British thinking was being crystallized by "a Pentagon fueled drive by U.S. defense and aircraft industries to make Europeans dependent on American weaponry."

"Ruthless high-pressure U.S. salesmanship of arms and aircraft" was choking Europe's defense industries, said the London *Daily Telegraph*, the bible of Britain's Conservatives.

Equally portentous, too, is the inner side of Europe's closing door against us. Led by Krupps, West German firms are shipping whole factories to various East European states to be operated on a fifty-fifty basis with the Communist governments concerned. At the same time these governments are moving strongly in the direction of greater economic liberalism. Their economists are shocked at the Communist strait jackets they once accepted. [The great speed of this movement in Czechoslovakia brought the Soviet crackdown in 1968, three years later.]

"With the thrust toward a grand new order in Europe so well under way," said de Borchgrave, "the question posed to Washington is where does it all leave the U.S.?" A part of the answer was found in a leading Belgian magazine which summed up the general drift neatly: "Why should coexistence be inapplicable in Southeast Asia? Why do Americans refuse the advice of their allies? Do they really believe that they have already become masters of the world? This will cost them dearly some day."

Indeed it already has. Don Cook, another competent observer in Europe, wrote to the *Los Angeles Times* on May 9, 1965, about all SEATO and NATO meetings, saying that they are now dominated "by a kind of anxious lobbying which winds up in an undignified and damaging head count as to who is still on the American side."

We must, therefore, begin to reckon now with the unthinkable rapidly coming to pass—our best friends in the world turning their backs upon us and facing toward the

East. We must foresee a rapid drawing together of Western and Eastern Europe, most probably in close association with the Soviet Union. It is not too soon, either, to think of the Soviet nuclear umbrella being extended over Western Europe, protecting for one thing the growing French nuclear deterrent.

It is a deeply disturbing thing to reflect that "America is becoming irrelevant" to Europe. This is the fruit of our obsession about containing rapidly evolving Communist societies, flinging our resources prodigally around the world in an effort to wall them in and to prevent revolution from occurring anywhere in the "free world" until, in President de Gaulle's words, on April 27, we have become "a state that might think of itself, because of its power, to be invested with supreme and universal responsibilities."

Also, as Washington's new determination to enforce a *Pax Americana* unfolds, we must expect that the proliferation of nuclear weapons, to which we have been so firmly opposed, will expand. If no weak country can be safe from American intervention, then all middle-sized countries will have to ponder the acquisition of nuclear deterrents of their own. Even the little ones must try to get under the cover of some non-American nuclear umbrella.[2]

---

[2] As cited in Chapter 7, the Soviet invasion of Czechoslovakia in 1968 changed this situation drastically.

Intervention in Santo Domingo

However, it will be said that even if Asia and Europe turn their backs upon us, we can still maintain control of the Western Hemisphere. Canada and Mexico will be defenseless, economically and otherwise, and Latin America can be held. Surely our power is sufficient for that.

That seemed likely, too, until a revolt broke out in Santo Domingo on April 24, 1965. The rebels were composed of both military and civilian groups who wanted to bring back to power Doctor Juan Bosch, who was ousted by the military six months after the end of the thirty-one year nightmare of the tyranny of Trujillo. There was steam behind the new rebellion, and many Americans were immediately in danger, especially from the civilians who had been armed. Accordingly, a United States Navy task force with one thousand five hundred Marines aboard arrived April 26 to protect and evacuate American citizens, one thousand one hundred of whom were removed the next day.

Succeeding waves of American troops brought their strength up to four thousand two hundred by April 29, and this figure rose rapidly to thirty thousand, which was far beyond the number required to complete the evacuation of the remaining Americans. The purpose of the big intervention was obvious. As *The New York Times* put it on May 3: "President Johnson reiterated that their sole mission was to protect and evacuate endangered Americans and other foreign nationals. Yet, every private briefing held for Congressmen and correspondents in Washington emphasizes that the primary aim . . . is to prevent 'another Cuba.' "

The *Times* added that "this is an understandable concern, but not one that should prompt a panicky display of power whenever any hint of Communist infiltration is reported."

Nevertheless, this is what had happened. Military intelligence had come up with the names of fifty-eight alleged Communists involved in the rebellion, and this was judged sufficient to justify a massive intervention, despite Article 15 of the Charter of the Organization of American States (OAS) which says: "No State or group of States has the right to intervene, directly or indirectly, for any reason whatever, in the internal or external affairs of any other State. The foregoing principle prohibits not only armed force but also any other form of interference or attempted threat against the personality of the State or against its political, economic and cultural elements."

Article 17 says also: "The territory of a State is inviolable; it may not be the object, even temporarily, of military occupation or of other measures of force taken by another State, directly or indirectly, on any grounds whatever."

This is the law, and in ignoring it our leaders did not even bother to inform the OAS of their intervention, much less to consult it.

The United States violated completely not only the basic law governing our relations with Latin America but also the United Nations Charter, which requires every signatory to report any alleged measures of self-defense "immediately" to the Security Council. When others brought the issue to that Council, the delegate from Uruguay pointed out, on May 4, 1965, the violation of both charters. He rejected the "despotism of the strongest," and denied the validity of the new "Johnson Doctrine."

The Johnson Doctrine

He referred to the ultimate affirmation of the *Pax Americana* which President Johnson had made on May 3, the day before. Declaring that Communist conspirators had taken over the rebellion, the President asserted that "the American nations cannot, must not and will not permit the establishment of another Communist government in this hemisphere." The next day he declared, once more: "We don't intend to sit here in our rocking chair with our hands folded and let the Communists set up any government in the Western Hemisphere."

In these all-encompassing terms, Mr. Johnson brought the Truman Doctrine to its ultimate proportions. From this day henceforth, no revolution is to be permitted anywhere within the reach of our power, unless it be a revolution engineered from the Right. But in a revolutionary age, any age, the great majority of revolutions come from the Left. All these will promptly be crushed, since they *might* turn Communist. This may be a small chance, but *no* chance can be taken. Some Communists will certainly be in every revolution from the Left, and some endangered regime, or United States intelligence agency, can always be counted on with total confidence to sound the Communist alarm. Then the might of the United States will drop from the skies and crash upon the beaches.

This is the role which our leaders chose for us in the world after our total victories in World War II. We would contain others; we would forbid revolutions. So President Johnson closed his address on May 2, 1965, about the Dominican intervention, as follows: "We do not want to bury anyone, as I have said so many times before. But we do not intend to be buried."

In these words Mr. Johnson unconsciously announced the end of containment and the beginning of Fortress America. The master of the richest and mightiest power on earth felt our burial threatened by another revolt on a little Caribbean island. The Red tide was moving in upon us, but "we will not be buried." "As long as I am President of this country we are going to defend ourselves," Mr. Johnson declared in all solemnity. Obviously, the great fear to which our leaders had yielded in the plenitude of our postwar power is closing in on them. After nearly two decades of rushing to ten-alarm fires they still keep breaking out, and our increasingly strenuous efforts to put out little fires continue to fan far bigger ones.

Anger in Latin America

The May 3 headline over the *Los Angeles Times* reporter's dispatch from Buenos Aires was accurate: ANGRY ANTI-U.S. WAVE SWEEPS LATIN AMERICA: ALL TYPES OF POLITICAL GROUPS FROM NORTH TO SOUTH JOIN IN CRY OF "INTERVENTION." Intervention by the United States, wrote George Natanson, is "a violently emotional issue." Reports from nearly all the Latin countries expressed the deeply rooted fear: "This could happen to us." The Chilean Foreign Ministry announced its "profound alarm." The press of a dozen countries, which he named, united in condemning the action of the United States.

Washington's success in pressuring the OAS to take over the Dominican operation, on May 6, at least formally, may blunt some of the poignantly revived fears of "The Colossus of the North." Yet this is the deepest fear in the Western Hemisphere. It has a century of intervention behind it, which the Latin-Americans believed had been ended by the Good Neighbor policy. Now suddenly the nineteenth century is back again.

Actually, of course, it is too late for the Johnson Doctrine. It may be enforced for a time around the Caribbean, and on the northern rim of South America, but in reality, as Eric Sevareid pointed out on May 6, 1965, the great countries of South America and several of the smaller ones are separated from us by vast areas of water, jungles, and mountains. They are farther away than Europe and are peopled by large expanding populations which live in increasingly revolutionary situations. Natanson reported from Chile on May 2 that the Chilean people are in a mood to break with the past. They prefer President Frei's revolution by legislation, "but they would accept Communism as an alternative if Frei fails."

Faced with the threat of North American repression, the Latin Americans may feel that they have no alternative but to combine in a great Latin American union, one strong enough to defend its independence. Fortunately, Vice President Humphrey had announced, on April 14, United States support for the economic integration of Latin America leading to a "Common Market for the Western Hemisphere." A week later a dispatch from Rio de Janeiro disclosed that Chilean President Frei was proposing the "political unity of all Latin America, with the exception of Communist Cuba." [3]

Now under the impact of the Johnson Doctrine, Latin America may move toward unity more rapidly than would have been thought possible before the Santo Domingo intervention. If such a union comes into being, also, it will be defensive against both our economic and military power. Once again, our union with a sister continent is likely to be rejected, and a united Latin America would certainly erect its own nuclear umbrella.

[3] *Los Angeles Times*, April 21.

Into Fortress America

It is, therefore, much too late for *Pax Americana* to succeed. Pursuance of this fearful dream can only lead rapidly into Fortress America. Indeed, as the events since February 7, 1965, detailed above, indicate, this process is already far along. With a wall of hatred raised against us in Asia and a wall of indifference toward us rising in Europe, we only required the hostility of Latin America to complete our self-imposed encirclement in Fortress America. Now a second decision in Washington, within three months, to use our huge military power, suddenly, to frustrate revolution in small nations, half a world apart, has supplied the necessary catalyst.

Our military power is unimaginable, but the idea of using it to regulate the conduct and determine the future of peoples around the world is self-defeating. And before Fortress America really closes around us we ought to think in deadly seriousness what it would be like to live inside it. We may be sure that it would be a prison for all those who love individual liberty, for dissent would be repressed even more rigorously than it is already in "consensus U.S.A." We must anticipate that the worst excesses of the McCarthy period would become the order of the day. We have enough resources to give ourselves a good living on an autarchic basis, but a much more restricted one. Profits would be far smaller, and business would have to be controlled far more rigorously in a world in which the outthrusts of our investments and much trade would cease.

It is not too late to avert this tragic end to the American Dream, and to stop our efforts to forbid social change anywhere in the world of which we disapprove. We ought to have learned by this time that the law of social evolution is inexorable and that it works to change even Communist societies, literally before our eyes. This law of change is the wave of the future, against which all of our dykes are built in vain. We may survive in Fortress America, surrounded by a great sea wall of distrust, but we cannot live and thrive in the world in opposition to it.

On the other hand, it is not too late to turn back from the *Pax Americana* which it is beyond our power to establish. It will take time to restore the thaw in our relations with the Soviet Union which had so greatly reduced world tensions. It will take much of the wisdom about which the President so often speaks to end our hostile encirclement of the new China and to establish trade and friendly relations with her, as the United States Chamber of Commerce recently urged. It will not be easy to win back the confidence of the Latin Americans again. "Decades were spent in creating a policy of nonintervention in the internal affairs of hemispheric nations," said *The New York Times* on May 4, 1965, "and time will be needed to heal the wounds." That is surely a strong understatement.

Will Our Conservatives Speak Out?

Nor will any of these life-giving things be done unless many powerful conservative interests make themselves heard in Washington, before it is too late. In 1965, the current rising of our intellectuals is magnificent, but in foreign affairs the President has allied himself with the extreme rightist forces that he had overwhelmed at the polls in November, and who will now hold him to enforcing his *Pax Americana*. Since the Administration also disregards its own great liberal following, it is a time for our true conservatives, who still have great power, to make themselves heard. Twice since February 6 the Administration has antagonized enormous numbers of people abroad, and each application of the American mailed fist accelerates rapidly the turning of the world against us. We simply cannot afford a third massive affront to the opinion of mankind. Yet the explosive defensive-offensive mentality now gripping Washington may produce it at any time.

Every real conservative ought to be deeply disturbed also by the rapid decline of our government's credibility. On April 23, 1965, *The New York Times* declared that it had been one of the "casualties of the war in Vietnam. Time after time, high-ranking representatives of government—in Washington and Saigon—have obscured, confused, or distorted news from Vietnam," said the editorial, adding that the blame "goes back to the Pentagon, to the State Department and the White House."

Then came Santo Domingo, and on May 9 David Kraslow reported to the *Los Angeles Times* from the scene a representative comment that "you just can't believe what you're told any more." It was an ugly situation. Some reporters had learned "by bitter experience in Saigon that they could not accept what American officials told them as the truth." Now it was "recurring in Santo Domingo." Thus "a most precious thing" was being destroyed, for *a government that does not have credibility* "*rules not by consent but by force.*"

When writers in the two largest and most influential newspapers in the United States agree that Washington's credibility is rapidly and progressively being destroyed, everyone should be able to see that these adventures in *Pax Americana* are corrupting the foundations of our democracy here at home. How much longer can we permit this to continue?

There is equally deep cause for alarm when Robert J. Donovan, head of the *Los Angeles Times* bureau in Washington, can describe, on May 9, 1965, "President Johnson's tornadic reaction" to the Dominican revolt. We cannot afford cyclonic action in the White House, even against little states abroad; for even if catastrophe is avoided the turning of the world's peoples against us cannot be.

Once before, the real conservatives of the nation saved it. In 1954, when a few powerful officials were pushing us into a preventive war with China, President Eisenhower was warned by "a flood of communications that descended on the White House from powerful institutions all over the country." These are the words of James Reston of *The New York Times* on April 27, 1954.

This pressure of the genuine conservatives ended the push toward a world war then. Today the twin dangers of a carefully escalated holocaust or the inexorable closing in of Fortress America are far greater, and time may be short.

Epilogue (written in 1969)

Three years later, in 1968, each effort of President Johnson to deescalate the Vietnam War or to negotiate was greeted by a rise in the stock markets, sometimes to record heights. This new development showed that the economic interests profiting from the war, and from their military-industrial complex ties, were only a minority, and that the large majority of businesses and investors felt their interests were being damaged. By that time the true conservatives saw, also, that the effects of the war were really imperilling the nation.

4

Policies Propelling The United States Toward an Attack on China*

1967

Prologue (written in 1969)

As the American bombing of North Vietnam continued through its second year, and the tide of our troops into the torrid jungles of South Vietnam soared toward half a million, the prospects of escalating the war into China were examined in this article.

It begins by projecting an American attack on China, to punish her for "aggression" in aiding North Vietnam, and examines the deadly doctrine of escalation which had

* Reprinted from *The Minority of One*, January 1967.

*led our leaders to attack North Vietnam for aiding the
rebellion in South Vietnam.*

*Several forces pushing Washington toward disposing
of China are examined and the question is posed: "Does
not such an attempt have to be made, fairly soon, unless
our pretensions in East Asia are curbed?" Conversely, is
a good neighbor policy toward China really unthinkable?*

It was utterly incredible that the humane, civilized,
democratic, Christian American people should attack the
Chinese people—the oldest and largest people on earth,
long suffering, exploited by Western imperialism for a
hundred years, but at last standing up in the world and
entering into the twentieth century. Yet the Americans
found themselves attacking China through a combination of factors which they failed to control.

Ideological Aversion

Throughout the American power structure there was
deep aversion to Communism, because it abolished private profits, and strong resentment that after World War
II China became a Communist giant instead of the
capitalist friend for which we had fought during the war.
All of the various elements of the powerful China Lobby,
especially the exiled Chiang Kai-shek regime and its
friends, also fed these emotions.

The Deadly Doctrine of Escalation

In the age of H-bombs and nuclear missiles it was obviously nonsensical to plan for any more big wars, but the devotees of power politics and war would not be defeated. They set to work, especially some gifted "civilian militarists," and produced the doctrine of carefully regulated and controlled "limited" war. We could still apply an infinite number of degrees of force, "conventional" first and nuclear if necessary.

In most cases we would gain our objectives without using nuclear weapons, but if not we would go right on playing the game—killing a big enemy city, for example, and losing one of ours, or calculating what objective would be "worth" losing fifty million of our people. All we had to do was get on the escalator and go as far as necessary.

Since this deceptive doctrine enabled our leaders to continue to play power politics all around the globe, they bought it for Vietnam, beginning with just a few military "advisers" and going up through many escalations until they had five hundred thousand American men in the steaming disease-ridden jungles of Vietnam—or was it a million before the attack on China?

The escalation in killing methods in Vietnam horrified the entire world. First there were the helicopters to carry several kinds of fire to the natives in the jungles, then all kinds of bombers, including the huge B-52s, dropping trainloads of bombs daily on Vietnam. This had gone so far that on August 6, 1966, our ace Airman, Major Kasler, just before his capture, flew over parts of North Vietnam and viewing the huge bomb craters he thought it looked just like the moon. Seeing not a single sign of life, he termed it "just dead country."

From the air, too, shiploads of napalm were dropped on Vietnam, villages and all, month after month, horribly burning and maiming and dooming to miserable, shortened lives those not fried to death. "Nonlethal" gases were freely used also, in quantities and places that killed people, especially the children and the old who also died from our systematic use of "weed-killer" chemicals, to destroy rice crops and defoliate trees. The fighting men got what food was left. All sorts of frightful "anti-personnel" bombs were used where it was thought there might be a few Viet Cong.

Before we escalated into China, over a million helpless refugees had been driven to the coastal regions—or was it finally three million? Every unthinkable method of killing had been used also, save only nuclear bombs—the last precious device in the armory of escalation—to the increasing horror of all mankind and to the rising discomfort of the good men of Washington who applied these therapeutic measures. Yet the little Vietnamese stubbornly continued to resist our best efforts to "persuade" them to desist from "aggression."

So there was finally nothing left to do but to extend our prophylactic bombing into China. They were plainly guilty of helping "the aggressors" in North Vietnam to defend themselves. Nothing remained except to open the book of escalation for China and take the first steps. The whole frightful agony in Victnam had to be ended some way.

Of course, our leaders merely did their obvious duty. They had to apply to China the prescriptions for Vietnam, only on a much vaster scale. What they had done in little Vietnam already exceeded by far our bombing records in the Korean War and World War II. Yet the bomb and napalm factories in the United States were roaring night and day, and it could be done also in China.

The steps laid down in the book of escalation were plain: (1) bomb first all the roads, railways, air fields, ports, etc. in China that are near North Vietnam; (2) be sure to destroy all their nuclear plants; (3) since Chinese troops are now streaming into Vietnam and Thailand on foot, bomb everything in Zone B, further north; (4) continue on to Shanghai and Peking if necessary; (5) have our full nuclear arsenal ready to use selectively if a psychotic explosion of wrath in the Soviet Union forces the Russians to aid China on a massive scale.

It was soon after this that history itself ended. The people in the Unidentified Flying Objects from other planets came in large numbers to view what the Americans had done, and as they surveyed what had been the United States, their comments were strangely similar to Major Kasler's just before his unexcelled bombing career ended: "It is just a dead country! See those huge craters! It looks just like the moon!"

The Incredible Deception

Many of the viewers from outer space wondered why the American people had permitted it all to happen and their seers told them why. The Americans had had an election in 1964 in which one of the candidates, named Goldwater, had convinced a huge majority of the Americans that he would be trigger happy if he ever got control of America's limitless destructive power. So he was resoundingly defeated, to the deep relief of all the other earth men, by a man named Johnson, who convinced people everywhere that he could be safely trusted with his fingers on the red button. Over and over again he promised the people, and all peoples, that "We are not going North" in Vietnam and "We are not going to engage in a land war in Asia!" He abjured especially, on September 25, 1964, getting "involved with a nation of 700 million people and becoming tied down in a land war in Asia."

But Johnson was really the greatest power practitioner which America had ever produced. Safely in office, he promptly went North, very soon after his inauguration. On February 7, 1965, the native rebels of South Vietnam blew up our barracks and bombers at Pleiku in South Vietnam, while the guards slept, and Johnson almost instantly ordered the bombing of North Vietnam. Actually, he did this mainly to save one of our successive client governments in Saigon from collapse, since it was already tottering to its fall. Then, as protest mounted at home and abroad, he declared on April 7, 1965, that "We will not be defeated. We will use our power with wisdom and restraint. But we will use it!"

He was on the escalation train that led straight on into the fiery furnace. But he drove it very carefully at first, selecting bombing targets himself and vetoing others, but always taking the next "necessary" step to establish his power in Southeast Asia. From this nothing could deflect him. The greatest political deception in American history was an accomplished fact. In 1964 the American democratic process had been falsified, perhaps fatally.

As Thomas B. Adams of Massachusetts, a direct descendant of two United States presidents put it: "By guile and by subterfuge the President has carried the nation into war without consent of Congress or debate in the Senate. Each step in the escalation of the war has been a denial of the official statements made at the taking of the previous step.[1]

Vietnamese Aggression Invented

It was, of course, a complicated business. Everyone who had watched the tragedy in Vietnam since 1945 knew that the rebellion in the South was solidly rooted in the United States-aided and supported tyrannies of our appointed dictator Diem.

Martin Nicholas compressed it into a paragraph in the June 1966 issue of *Viet-Report*, saying that during the

[1] *The New York Times*, August 18, 1966.

three years 1959–1962: "the brutality of the Diem tyranny revealed itself with unmistakable clarity. During this period began Diem's massive witch-hunts against all opposition; the *agroville* and strategic hamlet plans were put into operation, large-scale guerrilla warfare broke out, the National Liberation Front was founded. Diem's army tried to overthrow him, the most eminent non-Communist figures in Saigon protested against the regime and were imprisoned, and the first battalions of U.S. 'advisors' arrived."

Yet, to justify the bombing of North Vietnam, the fiction had to be invented that the trouble in the South was all due to orders and infiltration from the North. Therefore Mr. Johnson and his lieutenants solemnly referred, day after day until the end, to the North Vietnamese "aggressors." "The aggression" was a constant theme. This was because mankind has built up over the past century a very deep detestation for aggressive war, enshrined, for example, in the Briand-Kellogg Pact and the Nuremberg judgments. Our leaders *had* to transfer the guilt for aggression in Vietnam to the recipients of their mighty air assaults, lest they stand convicted before world opinion and some future Nuremberg tribunal— and to secure compliance with the war at home. The latter objective was largely achieved by massive repetition acting on the minds of conformist Americans, though no one was deceived abroad.

Colonialism did not smell any sweeter to Asia or the world when dressed up in the most solemn Johnsonian utterances. Vietnam was legally one country, expressly created as such by the great international treaty of 1954 which gave it its independence. It was therefore impossible for non-Americans, and a great number of Americans, to think of the North Vietnamese as aggressors in their own land.

The Rule of the All-powerful Three

The final American President was aided by two ideal lieutenants. Secretary of Defense McNamara was the ablest man ever to hold that impossible post. More than any of his predecessors he was able to control the generals and admirals, but the power of the vast military-industrial complex was too great for any man to manage. Aided by legions of government-supported scientists, it was always able to force through vast multi-billion appropriations for ever more miraculous "weapon systems," for crash programs to go to the moon and beyond, and for vast subterranean cellars in which to prolong for a few days the lives of America's elite when the nuclear holocaust came. McNamara occasionally had glimpses of the need to escape from this cycle of doom, but as he assured one televised hearing, "Somebody has to police the world" and he never doubted that he headed the apparatus for doing it.

Secretary of State Rusk was an adamant man, who was reputed to have had enough of China during the Korean War. He had a simple little litany about everything being all right in Vietnam if only the North Vietnamese will let their neighbors alone, which he repeated endlessly. And on televised hearings he indicated, with a straight face, that the multibillion-dollar American bases in South Vietnam—Army, Navy and Air—did not have any permanent importance. We had abandoned bases before. In all respects Mr. Rusk was the perfect Democratic Dulles, remaining absolutely firm about our supervisory role in the world. These three "strong" men—all good husbands and kind fathers—believed that they had the reins of world power in their hands and that they knew how to use them.

The President, at the top of the iron trio, rose rapidly to his global role. Even before the 1964 election, he had equipped himself with a Congressional resolution after the Tonkin Gulf affair, which gave him broad and vague authority to do anything he wished about Vietnam. Dulles had paved the way for him well on two previous occasions. In January 1955 he had secured from the Congress, by nearly unanimous votes, a resolution giving the President power to do anything he wished in the Formosa Straits. In January 1957 he had repeated this easy feat by securing blanket authority to use our armed power as he saw fit in the Middle East. So in August 1964, when in very cloudy circumstances a little North Vietnamese boat was alleged to have fired on two of our closely patrolling warships, it was easy for Johnson to get the Congressional sheep to approve another blank check for Vietnam.

Thereafter, he refused to admit that there were any

constitutional restraints on his power. He nullified the crucial power of Congress to declare war and when strong unrest arose in the Congress and the country, he went to Omaha in July 1966 to inform all dissenters that there are "many, many, many" who can recommend and advise, while "sometimes a few of them consent," nevertheless "there is only one that has been chosen by the American people to decide." His power to make war and peace had become "unlimited and arbitrary," as Walter Lippmann pointed out.

The method of operation of the all-powerful Three was simple. It was never to admit a mistake. In bleak contrast to President Kennedy's saving ability to do so and to change course, they blundered straight ahead, piling error on error. "Now when a mistake is made," said Thomas B. Adams, "another is made to blot out the memory of the previous blunder."

Growing Indignation at Home and Abroad

President Johnson had the power to destroy all the other peoples, without any voice or vote on their part, as historian Arnold Toynbee often protested. The President did not mean to do that, but his will to prevent any more popular uprisings anywhere lest they might turn Red, was made blazingly clear both in Santo Domingo and Vietnam. He took this central principle of the 1947 Truman Doctrine and made it a terrible reality.

Yet as the huge white man from across the world constantly beat and burned the little yellow boy in Vietnam, the gorge of all the peoples steadily rose. As the spectacle continued for eighteen months (or was it thirty-six finally?), the most illiterate man on any continent could understand what was happening. Aside from a few client regimes and oligarchical classes, all the world united in condemning what we were doing. Secretary General U Thant denounced it as "one of the most barbarous wars in history." Pope Paul often deplored it. The greatest religious organizations condemned it. Men of conscience everywhere knew that the Vietnamese had been struggling and dying for their independence for twenty years, against the Japanese, French and Americans in succession. People marvelled that they could continue to fight, but they did, and revulsion against the grisly spectacle was continual and manifestly rising.

Even at home there was unheard of protest. Students demonstrated from coast to coast, chanting: "Hey, Hey, LBJ! How Many Kids Have You Killed Today?" Professors conducted all night teach-ins to packed houses. The newspapers frequently carried full page protesting ads signed by hundreds of leaders. Religious leaders and bodies seethed, and gradually the Congress awoke from the shame of giving its birthright away. Senator Fulbright conducted televised hearings which questioned the whole tragic affair. Among courageous newsmen James Reston pointed out that "The bomber is not prevailing in Vietnam," but that the "war" was costing us "over 100 lives a week—to say nothing of the wounded and the diseased and the corrupted." [2]

What was happening to our men in Vietnam, and what they were doing to the Vietnamese people sickened an increasing number of Americans, who saw that our fire power was "smashing the social structure of the countryside." [3] Beyond that, our overpowering presence in South Vietnam was corrupting the whole Vietnamese people. The picture was "frightening: black marketeering, prostitution, corruption in even the highest levels of government, spectacular enrichment of the few while the mass of the people live in misery." Thoughtful Vietnamese watched "with horror as all the principles on which their society was constructed crumbled away," [4] and, as *The New York Times* revealed on August 14, 1966, authoritative military studies showed that seven hundred fifty thousand American troops would be required to suppress the Vietnamese, and from five to eight years. Later estimates raised the number to one million Americans required in South Vietnam, if the vital Mekong Delta is to be occupied.

Denis Warner, the highly competent Australian newspaperman, veteran of Vietnam, reported on August 24, 1966, that though we had already a million men on our side in Vietnam, they were "far from adequate to launch sustained offensives." More and more American men

[2] *The New York Times*, July 17, 1966.
[3] *The New York Times*, editorial, August 21, 1966.
[4] Max Clos, "The Karma of Vietnam's Buddhists," *The New York Times Magazine*, August 21, 1966, p. 90.

would be required. The war was, as Senator Mansfield had warned, "inherently open-ended."

Increasing Frustration and Desperation

So it was. It began to eat up the funds for the Great Society, President Johnson's great contribution. It diverted money most urgently needed to cope with our vast, festering, revolutionary cities, and from such things as the polluted air and putrid waters that threaten our very existence. It poisoned the national life and started the inflation humming that could bring about a calamitous homecoming of our huge international Cold War deficits held abroad.

Gradually realization spread through the Johnson Administration that it was in peril. From the White House down through the State and Defense Departments, the CIA, AID, and the Information Agency, all energies were concentrated on Vietnam. The ablest men from civilian agencies everywhere were "raided and engaged," wrote Max Frankel in a remarkable Washington report.[5] Up to 20 per cent of the personnel of major government offices was concentrated on Vietnam and they were usually "the top 20 per cent," as it was realized "throughout Washington that the war will make or break the entire Johnson Administration." The hot winds of coming

[5] *The New York Times*, August 11, 1966.

elections began to blow through Washington, but our world policemen clung to their simple faith that the red dominoes really would fall in Asia and everywhere unless we kept the bombers roaring and the troops flowing, and they assigned "great value to the war's contribution to the 'containment' of China." They scented recompense for all the agony if they could only prove that guerrilla wars could be smothered by fire.

At this stage, one could not quite say that the Johnson Administration was getting frantic, but as the debilitating, corrupting and frustrating struggle in Vietnam continued, it became more and more so. Always, too, the Washington finger pointed toward China. If only she would stop aiding her neighbors, the Vietnamese, to defend themselves. But she wouldn't. So finally Washington's patience gave out. It was six oil trucks, spotted by one of our planes, as they came across the Chinese border toward Hanoi which did it. This was too much. The temper of the man at the all-powerful controls gave way and he ordered that China's interference with our beneficent mission in Asia must be ended. China had become "an aggressor" and must be punished, even as North Vietnam had been, so frightfully, endlessly, and fruitlessly. The punishment, too, would have to fit the size of the culprit.

Will It Work Out Differently?

It may be that we shall not be led through the open-ended war into an effort to destroy everything in China that matters, even if hundreds of millions die. It could be that the will of the Vietnamese to resist us will finally collapse, just before we have to chastise China, but if this happens, the evil day has only been postponed. Our tremendous iron ring, drawn so closely around China, will have to be maintained.

Many busy, trusting Americans are not even aware of its giant posts: (1) six hundred thousand native troops in South Korea plus fifty thousand of our own men; (2) many armed American bases in Japan and the Philippines; (3) vast air and nuclear missile armaments on Okinawa Island, off China's central coast; (4) a half million Nationalist Chinese troops on Formosa, including some on islands in the mouths of China's harbors; (5) our giant bases in Vietnam and Thailand; and (6) the mightiest fleet that the world has ever seen, riding constantly off China's coasts.

Here is one of the world's most fantastic incredibles. Who could have believed that the ex-isolationist Americans would have done this? Yet who can doubt that this mighty encirclement of China is a sure prescription for disaster? If our leaders do not plunge on to destroy China now, can there be any question that she will push her nuclear armament as hard as she can to break out of our armed encirclement, as we or any other proud nation would? This will lead to a rising demand in high places here for nuclear attacks on China, before she has many nuclear missiles able to reach us. And, if this delayed attack on China does not take place, she will eventually evict us from her neighborhood, with or without a nuclear world war.

This is the course we are now on. The way is wide open, and very powerful forces in this country will urge us to stay on it.

It involves disaster for us, either way you look at it. If we wage a preventive nuclear war on China, we will be loathed by all the world's peoples, while the Japanese and other neighboring peoples would be in the path of the deadly fallout, which would also reach us. If China gets great nuclear armaments the outlook is no better.

Are We Capable of Being a Good Neighbor?

The alternative is to begin the slow and painful process of trying to make friends with China, to draw her out of her angry isolation, to bring her into the world community, even helping with the industrialization she so greatly needs. This involves remembering that she suffered from exploitation and humiliation by the West for a century before 1949. It involves gradual withdrawal from our great ring of encirclement. It means working toward a world community to which all the peoples belong—including the great Chinese nation, one of the most gifted peoples in the world.

By staying on the collision course we could spend another trillion dollars on our Cold War machine, perhaps two trillions over the next few decades, keeping wages and profits high until the end. The peaceful alternative would require great patience and probably more Christian fortitude than we possess, but it would enable history to continue.

Toward Genocide in Asia

Unfortunately, our rulers feel driven to foreclose any long-range evolution of our relations with China. The Johnson leadership will not live with Asia on any terms not imposed by Washington. On August 21, 1966, Chalmers Roberts of the *Washington Post* reported that "Washington today is grim and determined to see the war through." It was "the overwhelming view" that after surviving the November election the President's inclination will be "overwhelmingly to pour it on with everything he can," trying to keep the war inside Vietnam, and "to the fullest possible extent sooner rather than later." He will "prove to the skeptics that he has been right all along."

The President's now-revealed character justifies this appalling future prognosis. He is too power-possessed to understand how Charles de Gaulle rose rapidly to be the world's top statesman by taking France out of Algeria after a century of domination there, devastating the prestige of the French Army and bringing a million em-bittered French *colons* back to France. Today, no na-tional leader anywhere has prestige as high as de Gaulle's, and this is because doing what is right generates prestige.

Oblivious to such life-giving truths, the Johnson Ad-ministration can think of nothing but to step harder on the escalator. The President intends to crash through to some kind of "victory" before the 1968 election, all the while begging the victims of his variegated bombing campaigns to "come to the conference table," confess that they are "the aggressors," and join the Great Capi-talist Society.

But as the desperation of our rulers grows about the endless treadmill of death and devastation they are on, the determination of the American people to get us off must grow faster. We cannot afford to wait until we can get a change of presidents at the polls. It may be too late by 1968. With blind leaders controlling the engines of total destruction, we can easily find ourselves engaged in genocide in China long before 1972.

Stopping the escalator before we reach that abyss is the crucial consideration, but another is vital and related, for if our rulers succeed in crushing all patriotic dissent in distant countries, no matter how brutally, they will eventually suppress it here at home. Our own freedom is at stake in Vietnam!

Epilogue (written in 1969)

In December 1968 the likelihood of a war with China over Vietnam had greatly diminished, due to two complementary factors: (1) the American escalation was held under control; and (2) China was steadily weakened by the divsion and conflict attending the Cultural Revolution.

These developments relieved many deep anxieties. On May 13, 1967, Secretary General U Thant of the United Nations said that if the present trend continues, "I am afraid direct confrontation, first of all between Washington and Peking, is inevitable. I hope I am wrong, but I am afraid we are witnessing today the initial phase of World War III."

In a Senate speech on July 11, 1967, Majority Leader Mike Mansfield warned that we were "approaching a fork of the road in Vietnam." He feared the war would spread, engulfing Korea, the Formosa Strait, and China, and asked: "Who will say . . . that a third world war is not already incubating in the ever-deepening and expanding struggle in Southeast Asia?" A few weeks later, Senator Eugene McCarthy, of Minnesota, warned that "the Administration was escalating its objectives, a policy leading toward the ultimate escalation—developing an open confrontation with Red China." At the same time, October 1967, Wilfred G. Burchett, an Australian Communist correspondent, was assured "at the very highest level" in Hanoi that "China is ready to intervene at any moment," if more American troops were put in than North Vietnam could handle. "They are completely prepared for any eventuality." In Peking, he had been assured of the same thing. He was "as sure of this as I am of anything I have ever written." [6]

On December 29, 1967, James Reston of The New York Times summed up the risk-taking of the year as follows: "For twelve long months we risked a war with China that never came. That is something we couldn't be sure about, and we probably wouldn't tolerate it if China had a large bomber force on our borders. The truth is that we have not really had control of the issue of war with China all year long, but we got away with the risk and that is obviously a plus."

In January 1968 Edwin O. Reischauer, a leading Asian expert and lately ambassador to Japan, expressed the fear that "America is drifting perilously close to war with China over Vietnam"; and in the same month Han Suyin, a noted writer on China, was convinced that as things then stood a Sino-American war was inevitable. The Vietnam War was but a prelude to a United States assault upon China. On February 6, 1968, Eric Sevareid of CBS found in Mexico "a great uneasiness over our activities in Asia." There was new fear that the seizure of our spy ship Pueblo by North Korea might touch off a great war.[7]

Fear of war with China continued strong in early 1968.

[6] War/Peace Report, November 1967.
[7] CBS television and The New York Times Book Review, January 14, 1968, p. 22; January 28, p. 42.

On February 13 Joseph C. Harsch wrote in the Christian Science Monitor that "The outcome has to be either a major war between the great powers or a compromise"; and on February 19 Newsweek reported that "Many in Washington sense that the nation is being propelled toward a rendezvous with history in the scarred hills of a remote corner of Asia." A few days later, on February 25, Senator J. William Fulbright, chairman of the Foreign Relations Committee, issued his famous demand for a full scale reexamination of United States policy in Vietnam, "before a call for further troops takes the war to the China border and war with China," "and probably Russia too"; and in the ensuing committee hearings Senator Joseph Clark of Pennsylvania declared, on March 12, that "to go on as we are must inevitably end in a confrontation with China and perhaps World War III."

On February 19, 1968, Newsweek carried a great article by Emmet John Hughes denying that there was any analogy between the Vietnam War and any of our earlier wars. We had never been cast before as the heir to hated colonial authority, nor had we previously engaged in "the audacious labor of creating a new sovereignty." Also the crisis could already have become "appallingly more grave if China had not been locked in its own civil strife, if its schism with Russia had not widened, or if Communism were, in short, the monolithic menace of American mythology." We had been "incredibly lucky," but "there remains for us but to wonder whether a mindless reliance on reprieve-by-chance holds much promise of long life as a great power."

5

Vietnam and After*

1968

Prologue (written in 1969)

All through 1967 and the first quarter of 1968 our vast apparatus of annihilation continued to destroy the homes, livelihood, and lives of the Vietnamese people, North and South, but especially the latter. All the while, too, the conscripted levies of American youth continued to go to Vietnam and the casualties to mount until they approximated one thousand a week—the dead ranging from one hundred to three hundred—many of the wounded to linger on as permanent reminders of our effort to bring peace and freedom and free enterprise to Vietnam. The monetary costs climbed also until they exceeded $30 billion a year, driving us off the free gold

* Published in *The Western Political Quarterly*, March 1968.

standard, imperiling our internal economic stability and preparing the way for a new high level of "defense" expenditures after the war.

As the American agony lengthened interminably, revolt grew among the youth in the colleges, among their teachers, and among their elders. There were marches, demonstrations, sit-ins, and constant protests in full-page advertisements—sometimes even three pages filled with protesting signatures. The Senate Committee on Foreign Relations and other Congressional leaders rebelled, at the cost of being called "Nervous Nellies" by the President. Real rebellion flared in the great black ghettos of our cities, with much destruction of property, as hope of ever escaping from the degradation of living in them steadily declined.

The nation seethed with resentment while its good name plummeted abroad, yet the constant protests seemed to accomplish nothing. Nevertheless they continued, as our headquarters in Washington and Saigon ground out claims of progress in Vietnam.

In July 1967 a World Conference on Vietnam, called by the International Confederation for Disarmament and Peace, was held in Stockholm. It was attended by 350 delegates from 63 countries, on all continents. The conference divided into four commissions whose reports on various aspects of the struggle merged into an "Appeal to the World for Vietnam," which declared that "The American escalation in Vietnam has become nothing less than genocide."

The following address was delivered by the author at this conference.

American foreign policy in East Asia is a disastrous mixture of anti-Communist ideology, containing China as a great power; smashing guerrilla war, once and for all; economic imperialism; belief in our duty to police the world and in our invincible power; step by step involvement; and, finally, blind leadership. It must always be remembered, also, that all of these drives have behind them a vast military-industrial complex, ready at all times to supply the power and to profit from the successive wars of *Pax Americana*.

Manifest Destiny

Throughout our history we have faced west with great confidence. Beginning as colonials on our eastern seaboard in the early sixteen hundreds, we gradually subdued the mid-continent and took it from the Indians and the Mexicans. It was our Manifest Destiny, our leaders told us, and all believed it. Arriving at the Pacific Ocean we acquired Alaska and Hawaii and seized the Philippines from Spain.

Toward Europe we had an inferiority complex. We had fled from her shores, in great numbers, down to World War I, but we faced west with full confidence, so much so that the Texas frontiersman who now occupies the White House can rationalize his terrible predicament in Vietnam by talking expansively of our mission in Asia, even proposing to bring the Great Society to Asia, while it is withering at home.

Of course our Manifest Destiny is another term for American imperialism. A long-time friend of the United States, Sir Denis Brogan, accepted us as "the new imperial power" in a recent series of lectures. He did not discuss the powerful expansive forces generated by our dynamic economy, with immense profits constantly demanding investment and reinvestment, but he did find a great deal of our activity abroad to be "innocently imperialist in the sense that it does expect the world to turn American."

He warned also against our pre-Vietnam assumption of our omnipotence, saying: "The world cannot be made, by any exercise of American wisdom or power, a safe and agreeable place to live in. . . . There are many problems in the world which the American people did not create and cannot solve." He cautioned, too, that "the leaders of the new countries cannot be conjured out of the earth by the most massive doses of military aid or straight economic aid." [1]

[1] D. W. Brogan, *Worlds in Conflict* (London: Hamish Hamilton, 1967), pp. 5, 33, 57, 60, 126.

Pax Americana

Nevertheless, there can be no doubt that, until recently at least, our leaders felt it to be their duty to police the world, certainly the "free world."

All possible doubt about the determination of the Johnson Administration to suppress any violent outbreak of social discontent anywhere in the "free world" was removed by the Pentagon's current proposal to build a fleet of thirty FDLS—"fast deployment logistic ships." Each would be filled with heavy military equipment for two divisions—helicopters, trucks, mobile guns, etc.—to be stationed in harbors or cruising around the world, ready to dash to any "trouble spot" to meet the C-5A jumbo jet transport planes that will be ready in two years to carry seven hundred American troops each and rain them down wherever discontent raises its head.

Fortunately, that impeccable conservative, Senator Richard B. Russell, chairman of the Senate Armed Services Committee, has blocked this fully revealing proposal, for the time being, telling the Senate on March 21, 1967, that "we should not unilaterally assume the function of policing the world. If it is easy to go anywhere and do anything, we will always be going somewhere and doing something." Nothing could be more painfully evident, but Senator Russell's time in the Senate is short and the Pentagon, from McNamara on down, is determined to press the proposal in succeeding Congresses. Only a national rising of disillusioned citizens can really block this final preparation to forbid forever all revolution in the "free world," lest it turn Red or expropriate our properties.

Since the vast underdeveloped world will seethe increasingly as its social problems grow more acute and since other peoples will continue to assert their right to settle their own problems, nothing but a national decision to turn off the Imperial Way can avert a long series of Vietnams.

Containing China

American policy toward East Asia has been dominated since the end of World War II by deep disappointment over the Communist takeover in China and by a firm determination to "contain" both Chinese Communism and China as a great power. Stimulated by the Korean War we have built a tremendous ring of armed power of every kind around China—in South Korea, Japan, the Philippines, Okinawa, Formosa, Quemoy and Matsu, and now in South Vietnam and Thailand—backed by the immense strength of our Seventh Fleet, constantly patrolling China's coasts. This mighty encirclement, supported by an attempted economic and diplomatic blockade of China, has not unnaturally produced an angry, sullen dragon, convulsed with a great effort to maintain its Communist purity and pushing its atomic and nuclear armaments with astonishing speed.

Red Monolith

The American attempt to contain and confine the most numerous and perhaps the most gifted people on earth was grounded originally in the belief that the entire Communist world was a giant monolith, commanded and directed by a superbrain in Moscow. This was never true, but the idea persisted even after the death of Stalin, early in 1953, and long after the rapid splitting apart of Russia and China was evident. Long after the separate evolution of Communism in each East European Communist state was manifest, beginning with Yugoslavia in 1948, our leaders continued to talk of "the Communist conspiracy." As late as January–February 1966 Mr. Rusk was talking about "the Communists" and "their world revolution." [2]

It became constantly clearer that the law of social evolution is inexorable and that it works relentlessly in both communist and capitalist countries, yet we clung to the myth of the Red Monolith. This was because there was continuing fear of communist power and because the communist abolition of private profits was regarded as the ultimate sin which must be eternally fought, since

[2] Arthur M. Schlesinger, *The Bitter Heritage: Vietnam and American Democracy* (Boston: Houghton Mifflin Company, 1967), p. 68.

any extension of Communism contracted the area in which private profits could be freely earned.

Vietnam

It followed that after World War II the people of Vietnam could not be permitted to win their war of independence from France, because they had Communist leaders. We therefore poured nearly $3 billion worth of military and economic aid for France into Vietnam, and Secretary of State Dulles did all that one utterly determined man could do to prevent France from making peace. When he failed he refused to accept the Geneva settlement of 1954, which divided Vietnam purely for the temporary purpose of liquidating the war, and our government worked to make the division permanent.

This had three effects: (1) it frustrated independence for the South Vietnamese; (2) it reimposed a feudalistic social system on the South Vietnamese peasants, involving the restoration of hated landlord rule; and (3) our Mandarin tyrant Diem plunged the country into bitter and widespread revolt.

After his fall, other alleged "governments" in Saigon failed and in desperation President Johnson began the bombing of North Vietnam on February 7, 1965, alleging that the whole trouble was due to North Vietnamese "aggression." It was claimed that the trickle of aid in men and supplies coming to the aid of the rebels in South

Vietnam constituted aggression against the separate nation of South Vietnam by the Vietnamese of the North. A civil war in the South, for which we were responsible, was alleged to be a case of international aggression.

This is the great myth under which the tragedy of Vietnam grinds on. There is no nation in South Vietnam, either legally or actually. There are the old possessing classes, the seven hundred thousand Catholic refugees from North Vietnam who came south after 1954, liberal patriots in the cities who want a new order, and the peasant majority which wants no more tyranny from Saigon. Certainly the bulk of the people want Vietnamese independence and liberation from the corrupt and reactionary South Vietnamese Army, which fights so little and deserts so freely. It is highly significant that only one officer in this army above the rank of lieutenant colonel did not fight on the side of the French during the war of independence.[3] All the others did, including General Ky, and to the Vietnamese nationalists they are all traitors, doubly so because they now fight with us.

War for Independence

That the great majority of the Vietnamese are still fighting for their independence is clear to most observers. United Nations Secretary General U Thant has no doubt

[3] Jonathan Randall, from Saigon, *International Herald-Tribune*, June 12, 1967, p. 7.

about it. Nationalism, not Communism, inspires the resistance, he says, and "the war cannot be brought to an end until this fundamental fact is recognized." [4]

Nothing less than a burning nationalism could have sustained the Vietnamese, South and North, under our daily bombing for the past two and a half years, during which incredible tonnages of bombs and bullets, napalm and crop destroyers—every kind of fire except atomic—have been dropped on them.

As the spectacle has unfolded, few people abroad have been able to believe that the little brown people under the bombers are aggressors in their own land. Yet no government, however mighty, can admit that it is an aggressor, and our leaders have called the North Vietnamese "the aggressors" so long that they may believe their own charge by this time.

Blind Leaders

To believe otherwise is to admit their own blindness and ineptitude. Johnson and Rusk, McNamara and the generals—all had seen the indecisive and counter-productive effects of the wholesale bombing of Germany from 1941 to 1945. They had all observed during the Korean War that the lines of communication of an Asiatic army in favorable terrain could not be destroyed by bombing. With total control of the air over North Korea we could

[4] *International Herald-Tribune*, April 28, 1967.

not do it. Yet they blindly and confidently tried to do the same thing in Vietnam.

Even from the standpoint of self-preservation as leaders, they might have remembered that the Korean War put the Democrats out of power in Washington in 1952, and purely as a skilled politician Johnson might have seen the unwisdom of making the Democrats "the war party" for the fourth time in this century. If they thought about these things at all, they must have decided that the destructive power at their command was now so tremendous that they could not fail.

Escalation

Besides, they had the new theory of escalation. All you had to do was to start the escalation machine and keep it running until the adversary yielded. They never thought that a little Oriental people would fight on to the point of annihilation, a point which is now visibly in sight, as *The New York Times* warned recently.[5]

In the early days of the bombing of North Vietnam it was frequently suggested in Washington that they would soon "get the message," but they didn't. As the weeks wore on, President Johnson made a formal address, on April 7, 1965, in which he declared in the most absolute terms that his will must prevail. Mr. Johnson is a proud man. Indeed, Walter Lippmann, the distin-

[5] Andrew Kopkind, "Report from Washington," *New Statesman*, May 5, 1967, p. 606.

guished dean of American journalism, believes that "the root of his troubles has been pride, a stubborn refusal to recognize the country's limitations or his own limitations. Such pride goeth before destruction . . . and an haughty spirit before a fall." [6]

The same sense of deep foreboding is shared by the Reverend Eugene Carson Blake, General Secretary of the World Council of Churches, who says that in Vietnam we are moving "step by step to tragic disaster." We cannot win, he says, regardless of the number of "successful air strikes and clean-up operations we complete," since each step increasingly isolates us from the rest of the world and falsifies our ideals. "Month by month and year by year we strengthen our foes as we use more violent power against them. Everybody in the world sees it, protests it and is ignored as we push on blindly to disaster." [7]

We are in the midst of a spectacular demonstration of the ancient maxim that "where there is no vision the people perish."

But to stop the bombing without bringing Ho Chi Minh bruised and bleeding to the conference table would be a confession of failure for Mr. Johnson and his aides, so they periodically stage peace offensives, sending missions all over the world to plead for someone to negotiate with. I want to negotiate, the President complained on April 27, 1967, "but I can't negotiate with myself." [8]

[6] The Observer (London), May 21, 1967, p. 11.
[7] International Herald-Tribune, April 28, 1967, p. 2.
[8] Ibid.

Of course it has long been evident that he cannot get negotiations without stopping the bombing, definitely, and he will not do that unless Hanoi will agree to stop supporting its troops in South Vietnam. This, in turn, is something that no undefeated government could do, as Senator Charles Percy pointed out in an outstanding speech on April 22. He condemned as unrealistic the demand to Hanoi "virtually to abandon its forces in the South." [9]

To End All Guerrilla Wars

So the bombing of North and South Vietnam thunders on, and there is a further reason why it must. Washington is determined to prove that guerrilla-based wars cannot succeed. Vietnam's General Giap defeated the French by this method. Mao Tse-tung won China by it and under the spur of our encirclement China has planned a campaign to defeat capitalism throughout the hungry Southern Hemisphere by guerrilla action. Therefore, it is said, the issue must be decided now. Washington cannot admit that its incredibly mechanized arsenals of destruction can be defeated by little Vietnamese men on the ground, fighting with what they can carry.

Arthur M. Schlesinger, Jr., writes that our tragic entanglement in Vietnam is not due to deliberate consideration, "but through a series of small decisions" when

[9] *The Guardian* (Manchester), April 24, 1967.

each proposed step plausibly promised success, and when other high priority crises claimed attention.[10] There is undoubtedly a great deal of truth in this. Yet certain decisions have been long range and decisive.

The determination of Mr. Dulles and his aides to prevent the independence of Vietnam under Communist leadership was crucial, and every succeeding administration has sustained it. Similarly, President Kennedy, who knew well that each small step in Vietnam was "like taking a drink," nevertheless took several. In particular he was determined to work out methods of defeating a guerrilla war and he instituted a vast apparatus of counter-insurgency training against guerrilla action which presently attempts to train the free world against insurgency.

This whole concept is now at stake in Vietnam, or at least the Pentagon thinks it is. So the Vietnamese fight on with "idealism and dedication" against the "galling status quo" in Saigon which is the creation of Washington, to quote Neil Sheehan, ace correspondent of *The New York Times* in Vietnam.[11]

[10] Schlesinger, *op. cit.*, pp. 22–23, 31.
[11] Schlesinger, *op. cit.*, pp. 44–45.

America in Vietnam

What we are doing in Vietnam has been indelibly recorded in a series of articles by Mary McCarthy.[12] She found the American presence simply overwhelming— Saigon full of Western cars and white men, cheap new office buildings rising, hardly anything native to buy but every kind of American goods—a giant PX by day and pseudo-World's Fair at night. In the villages she saw zealous young Americans, all indoctrinated to believe that North Vietnam is "the aggressor," engaged in spreading the American way of life, especially free enterprise. American aid was being "applied, first of all, to achieve stability, that is, political stability for the present ruling groups," which had always been corrupt. Everywhere she heard the same stories of graft and corruption at the expense of the poor.

From the air she saw the country dotted with fires and burned-over areas, from the bombing, noted plane and helicopter crews "alert for the slightest sign of movement below" and marveled that the Anglo-Saxon sense of fair play had so atrophied. If a Viet Cong threw a bomb, that was an atrocity, but if an American bombed civilians in a village their deaths were *always* accidental. "Each time it was an accident." An estimated one quarter of the

[12] First published in the *New York Review of Books*. Reprinted in *The Observer* (London), April 30, May 7, and May 14, 1967.

peasant population would be killed or die of war-related causes.

Her overall conclusion was that "the worst thing that could happen to our country would be to win this war," and a similar conclusion has been reached by Senator McGovern, one of the most clear-sighted and courageous men in American life today. "Vietnam," he says, "is degenerating into a defeat for America whether we 'win' or 'lose' on the battlefield. . . . Our deepening involvement in Vietnam represents the most tragic moral failure in our national experience. This mightiest nation in history . . . is, with allegedly good motives, devastating an impoverished little State and ravishing the people whose freedom we would protect. . . . We are being pulled step by step into a jungle quicksand . . . a fearful path which our ablest generals have warned against for decades." There was, continued McGovern, "no American interest, no issue of political freedom, no moral imperative for sending our troops and bombers into Vietnam" and "no reason for placing our power in opposition to basic historical forces, including the current revolutionary nationalism and social ferment which is convulsing most of Asia." [13]

This is a stern judgment but a just one. President Johnson and his aides have shamed and disgraced us, a Christian people, by surpassing the worst days of European colonialism. They have professed to defend the freedom of the South Vietnamese against Communist regimentation, while fostering in Saigon an incredible

[13] *The Guardian* (Manchester), April 26, 1967.

mixture of corruption and misrule. They have brought to a devastating conclusion the doctrine issued by President Truman forbidding all popular revolutions, lest they might turn Red.

Talking liberty when their purpose was power, they have denied the American dream itself. The principle that every people has a right to revolt against oppressive government is the very taproot of American history, and the beacon light which has guided all men until lately.

Tragic Awakening

Fortunately, the American people are awakening to the full enormity of the disaster into which they have been led. In June 1967, Anthony Carew, chief foreign correspondent of the conservative London *Daily Mail*, made a six thousand-mile tour of the United States and published his findings on June 13th and 14th. Everywhere he saw the agony of a people "who have been half led, half pushed" into policing the world. All over America one heard the questions: "How long can it go on? Where can we draw the line?" The "terrible embroilment in Vietnam" was "reaching out its jungly fingers and touching the lives of every ordinary American" and "the prospect of this sort of thing being extended indefinitely and in many parts of the world was appalling everyone." It was "clear that Americans of all types and races and political opinions are beset by doubt and a sheer un-

complicated fear of what their nation has taken on. . . .
They question the whole role America has assumed. . . .
For many the Great American Dream has turned into
a nightmare.

"America," Carew's report continued, "is a divided
nation. The most powerful country in the world is presently engaged in a kind of moral civil war, and the damage now being done to the very fabric of America will
take generations to repair—if it can ever be repaired."
"Every American," he added, "whoever he is and whatever he is, is obsessed with Vietnam. It colours his thinking on other matters, warps his judgment and twists his
attitude to the rest of the world." However it ended, he
predicted that Vietnam will be "the costliest war in history," as "the expenditure of blood and cash and human
spirit mounts higher each day." Outside Washington
"the enormity of what the Vietnam mess is doing to
America is everywhere apparent. And . . . there are many
sensible men who can discern, not too far away, an
America physically exhausted and morally bankrupt."
Those who had always considered the bombing inde-
fensible were now joined by others who see that it is not
even successful, but they were being attacked by a strong
revival of McCarthyism.

In Washington, Carew reported that "the White
House lies in a torpor," with no apparent policy except
to stumble on, without realizing or caring that "America's spiritual credit is lower in the world than it has ever
been." The Administration was "a body of tired, spent
men, more interested in saving face than saving South-

east Asia from Communism." The President was "tragically out of his depth."

One must have a modicum of pity for Mr. Johnson as a human being, as the great Escalation Machine which he started so suddenly and so confidently destroys so much of Vietnam, along with so much that was promising in American life. But unfortunately he has shaken confidence in the democratic process itself by gaining election, overwhelmingly, as the man who would not escalate the war in Vietnam and then promptly proceeding to do so.

The Military-Industrial Complex in Control

It has to be recognized also that there are very powerful forces which are committed to subduing Vietnam. In his Farewell Address as President, General Eisenhower warned in all solemnity that America might come to be dominated by what he called the military-industrial complex, a union of the military officers and the great industrial and business interests which profit from war contracts. He saw its influence extending into every government office—national, state and local.

Today the military have their prestige committed to "winning" in Vietnam and the war contracts are bringing great profits and high wages to their allies in industry and business. This combination of interests is so powerful that it would require a very strong President to overrule it. As Eisenhower recognized, this is a permanent problem of great gravity. Senator Fulbright said recently, the military-industrial complex considers Vietnam to be "a nice little war—not too much killing, but a big help to the economy." [14]

Nevertheless, in early May 1967, a staff report of the Senate Republican Policy Committee was highly critical of our involvement in Vietnam, concluding that we were really fighting Vietnamese nationalism. It was reliably reported that the report represented "the feeling of a powerful 'coalition' of conservative politicians and moderate financiers and businessmen that the war may quite possibly ruin the country, and that it most certainly threatens their economic and political interests." It is possible that this group sees that the dominance of the military-industrial combination represents "a real and present danger of disaster." [15]

Never Again?

There is hope, too, in the reaction of the American people to the onset of the Israeli-Arab war. The London *Sunday Telegraph* reported, on May 28, 1967, that "nearly every American was in some degree hawklike (about the Middle East), but the consensus was that, after Vietnam, there must never be another lonely cru-

[14] *International Herald-Tribune,* May 5, 1967, p. 1.
[15] Kopkind, *op. cit.,* p. 606.

sade." General Eisenhower had added his oracular voice to this thesis.

What was lacking, said David S. Browder of the *Washington Post*, was moral leadership in the presidency, the voice of wisdom that would "utter some of the truths this sorely tried, angry and guilt-ridden country needs to hear, if it is to save itself from the quicksand of fear, distrust, selfishness and hypocrisy in which it is sinking." [16]

What Future?

If we are to make a real turn away from a succession of Vietnams and rapid national decline, it will have to be through the acceptance of principles such as these:

1. *That a lasting settlement for Vietnam involves:*
   (a) A stoppage of American efforts to control it. This does not mean a sudden withdrawal.
   (b) An announced willingness to negotiate with the National Liberation Front (the Viet Cong) and to admit it to a significant role in a provisional government.
   (c) Elections strongly supervised by the United Nations to produce a much more broadly based government, one not controlled by the generals and capable of preventing the

[16] *International Herald-Tribune*, May 26, 1967.

restoration of feudalistic misrule over the peasants. After these ancient abuses have been ended in China and North Vietnam they cannot be preserved in South Vietnam.

(d) A willingness to permit such a government to work out its own arrangements with North Vietnam for renewed intercourse and for an eventual federal union. There is strong evidence that the NLF itself does not desire any sudden one-sided union with the North.

(e) The United Nations presence in the transition period should be strong, to assist in the settlement of millions of helpless uprooted refugees and to supervise the withdrawal of foreign forces.[17]

2. *The United States has no mission to enforce a world* Pax Americana. The two world wars have destroyed Western imperialism and it cannot be restored. Nor can Communist imperialism make headway. The rivalry of democratic-capitalism with Communism precludes a world police role for either. If the world is to be policed, it must be done by a strengthened United Nations.

3. *It is not necessary for American capitalism to suppress social discontent or revolt throughout the "free world" in order to progress.* It can find ways of doing business with new regimes, even Communist ones. Euro-

[17] I have drawn considerably on Senator McGovern's excellent four points for a settlement.

pean capitalists are doing it successfully. Moreover, our own country still needs vast capital expenditure, especially for socially useful purposes. The backlog of needs for reconstruction at home is immense.

4. *Our country must solve the problem of living with the new China* in a mature, long-visioned manner. Though she appears to be a very dangerous neighbor now, she must gradually be brought into the world community and made a part of it. We must also relax our military encirclement of her in time to make it unnecessary for her to force her way out a decade or two hence, at the cost of the final world war.

In a far-sighted current article Alastair Buchan, director of the British Institute for Strategic Studies, foresees a future decision by India and Japan "to take Sino-Asian relations into their own hands." He does not suggest any role for the United States in managing Asia, a natural omission, since every Asiatic people knows that it must find ways of living in peace with the awakened, rapidly developing Chinese giant.[18]

5. *There is still a great role for the United States to play in the world,* as a leader in organizing it for peace and in united action to meet the crucial problems of ghetto living, hunger, underdevelopment and exploding populations, which menace all humanity.

[18] Alastair Buchan, "How the Asians Will Live with China," *The Times* (London), May 12, 1967.

Epilogue (written in 1969)

At the Stockholm Conference Gunnar Myrdal, the world-famous Swedish sociologist, said: "There is not a single government in Western Europe that would dare to send a single squad of soldiers to Vietnam as a symbolic gesture of sympathy with United States policy there," not even the dictatorships of Spain and Portugal—a verdict which was poignantly confirmed to this writer frequently. For example, a Danish college girl when asked about Vietnam replied, in evident pain, that she had spent a year in the United States and had considered it her second home, "but now a great gulf has opened between us and I doubt that it will ever close again." Likewise, a fine Chinese boy in Scotland, a refugee from Chinese Communism, replied to the same question: "I used to regard America as the home of liberty and self-determination and thought I would like to live there, but now nothing could induce me to go there."

We are daily destroying our leadership in the world and a strong leader without followers is "a dangerous aberrant," said Myrdal, as he warned that "literally trillions of dollars will have to be spent, and spent soon" to rebuild our ghettoized cities, "if America wants to prevent a breakdown of its social order and the loss of political democracy." No warning could be more grave.

Yet in early February 1968 there was no sign that our current leaders knew how to escape the bloody Asiatic quagmire into which they had walked so confidently.

Britain's devaluation of the pound led to hasty measures to avert the same fate for the dollar, due to our incessant Cold War international deficits for twenty years. But would the measures be effective? Inflation continued, speculation on our stock markets was massive, and there were fears of another world depression, fears not alleviated by the crash of an H-bomb laden United States bomber near Greenland, on one of those incessant patrols to deter Soviet attack, or by the capture of a United States Navy spy ship and crew by North Korea.

After months of predictions that "the Communists" would simply fade way in Vietnam, they were attacking in strength in Saigon and a dozen other cities in South Vietnam, and in provincial towns from one end of it to the other. Saigon was being bombed daily by the Americans, plunging into angry grief the great numbers of people who had fled from the bombers to Saigon for safety.

As a trauma greater than we had suffered in either of the two world wars gripped our own people, Esquire carried in December 1967 the warning of General Matthew B. Ridgway that "we commit ourselves to an upward spiraling course that may approach annihilation," and the admonition of General David M. Shoup, former Commandant of the Marine Corps, that "if we would keep our dirty, bloody, dollar-crooked fingers out of the business of these nations, so full of depressed, exploited people, they will arrive at a solution of their own." This is a harsh appraisal of our conduct, but one that is shared by the vast majority of mankind.

Trying to look ahead, the New Republic declared on January 27, 1968, that we should be planning now for "what comes next—beyond imperialism—a non-coercive, collective social and economic effort by the advanced nations that can give real hope of progress to the newer nations."

But can we get leaders who will go that way, while there is still time?

6

Vietnam and the Crashing Dominoes*

1968

Our entanglement in Vietnam has become the greatest
fiasco in our entire history. This is because the whole
adventure has been based on a series of false assumptions,
and unless they are clearly and strongly understood we
may go on into a national and world disaster.

Fortunately, President Johnson's decision not to stand
for reelection and to move toward peace gives us a chance
really to change course. Until he made this decision we
appeared to be set to ride the escalation train on into
the fiery furnace. Now, as we pull back from this prospect, it is imperative to understand the mirages of the
past which our leaders have been pursuing. *The Wall
Street Journal* did not speak a moment too soon when it

* Reprinted from *New World Review*, Summer 1968.

warned on February 23, 1968, that "the whole Vietnam effort may be doomed" and that "no battle and no war is worth any price, no matter how ruinous."

Our Illusions

The main illusions that have carried us to the point of facing the worst trauma in our national life are:

1. *That South Vietnam is a prize strategic spot.* This was a powerful idea in Washington in 1954 and there is some truth in it, if we are to assume the role of world policeman. But the day when coaling stations (or air bases) around the world can control it is gone forever. After the collapse of the old empires, aided by the mighty yeast of our own doctrine of self-determination, the former colonial peoples will never again submit to white control.

2. *The Dulles illusion that we could negate the decision of the Geneva Conference of 1954 and create a state in South Vietnam where none existed.* His motive was anti-Communist but the living body of Vietnam was cut in two, and nationalism is far stronger than Communism. Indeed Communism has become the vehicle for nationalism in Vietnam.

3. *The illusion that we could defeat Communism in South Vietnam by propping up a small corrupt landlord class that had already been largely ousted by Ho Chi Minh's first war of independence against the French.*

This effort guaranteed rebellion against our tyrant Diem which the North Vietnamese tardily supported. After feudalistic misrule has been ended in China and North Vietnam it cannot be preserved in the South.

4. *That we were containing an aggressive Chinese dragon.* This is a primeval assumption, but where is the evidence? The Chinese have asserted their long-recognized sovereignty over Tibet and rectified a strange border with India, after provocation. They have made reasonable border settlements with Burma and Thailand and helped North Korea and North Vietnam. Moreover, Vietnamese nationalism, especially in a united Vietnam, is a better bulwark than American occupation, veiled or otherwise.

Our vast armed encirclement of China—in North Korea, Japan, the Philippines, Okinawa, Taiwan, South Vietnam and Thailand, plus our mighty Seventh Fleet—is the most astonishing and quixotic adventure in our history. Unless the policy and state of mind behind it are changed, we must expect to find ourselves eventually either in a great "limited" war we cannot win or in the final nuclear war. As the new China grows stronger no other expectation is even semi-prudent. We need only to ask ourselves what we would do if the Chinese treated us the same way.

5. *The illusion that our bombers could enforce our will.* It is hardly believable that President Johnson and his advisers, military and political, should decide that just the right amount of bombing would put things in order in Vietnam. They had all lived through the Korean

War and witnessed the inability of all the bombing we could do to win, and they had also seen the Korean ordeal oust the Democrats from power. Yet they shut their eyes tightly and took that dolorous road again, expecting the Vietnamese to "get the message" in about three months.

So the North Vietnamese were attacked for helping, a little, their hard-pressed brothers in the South, and their aid to the rebellion in the South promptly became important and grew in strength during more than three years after we began the bombing on February 7, 1965. The people of the North, few as they are, rose in mighty resolution not to be bombed into submission and the daily evidence of our bombing defeated in men's minds around the world our constant assertions that we were not doing anything aggressive. It was the North Vietnamese who were "the aggressors!"

6. *That the failure of all guerrilla wars would be demonstrated.* This was the faith that sustained our leaders. It appeared to justify in their minds the "conventional" bombing of whole regions, the dreaded anti-personnel bombs, the dreadful use of napalm by the shipload, the dropping of phosphorus bombs that are even worse, the use of chemicals to kill crops and forests which also killed people, the killing of whole villages, the spraying of wide areas with machine gun bullets at night, the heavy use of helicopters, tanks, artillery and naval guns— all to prove that our immense arsenals of "sophisticated" weapons could put down any guerrilla revolt.

7. *The illusion that the domino theory won't work*

in reverse. From Truman to MacArthur to Johnson we
have been taught incessantly that if one little country
"goes"—Greece, Korea or Vietnam—the standing non-
Communist dominoes will fall against each other, crash-
ing all around the world, even across the oceans to our
own shores. We have been taught constantly that if we
don't defeat "them" over there "they" will soon be over
here, and many a fine boy has died in Vietnam believing
it, years after inexorable evolution destroyed the whole
notion of a huge Red Monolith working to destroy us.
Yet our leaders acted on the assumption that a Red
domino could be attacked by us with impunity, on the
other side of the earth.

8.   *That we could pulverize an ancient, viable civilization in Vietnam and erect a gleaming new capitalist
democracy there.* None of our assumptions is more deeply
disturbing than this. The horrors of this process, the corruption and degradation of millions of lives, including
so many of our own, the millions of piteous refugees
there and the growing threat that our democratic liberties
will be suppressed at home—all militated against success.
Yet our own national life is already warped by the attempt, enough to warn us that we shall lose here what we
try to impose on others.

We lay ourselves open also to the growing belief that
what is really at stake is preservation and expansion of
our economic empire.

9.   *The illusion that our prestige demands victory.*
This is said to be a life-and-death matter. We are the
greatest power on earth and we cannot confess failure.

This is because we have "commitments" to forty nations. They are all looking to us for protection and if we fail one of our clients all will lose faith in us. Surely this involves our sacred honor and our self-preservation.

Boomerang Dominoes

All of these assumptions have been proved to be illusions. It is late in the twentieth century. Two world wars have demolished the empire business and exposed the white man's feet of clay. Our own doctrine of self-determination has won the world and it cannot be frustrated abroad under the guise of an anti-Communist crusade. Even in the Communist areas of the earth neither the Soviet Union nor China can suppress the constant evolution of all states in their spheres of interest toward greater and greater freedom. The law of change is inexorable and the power of nationalism will not be denied.

Neither can our worst engines of death prevail over the human mind, body and spirit, when all three are united to defend national independence or to escape from intolerable privation and misrule at home. Nothing short of genocide can conquer people who are determined to be men. It is the saddest thing in our national record, too, that we have been destroying the Vietnamese people wholesale in order to "save" them for our purposes.

For three years we bombed everything in North Vietnam that might conceivably have military value, except perhaps the main Haiphong docks; destroyed villages in the South and their inhabitants at will; and finally largely destroyed the Southern cities "to save them." Yet our opponents became stronger than ever and all our efforts to pacify the people forcibly failed.

From the standpoint of maintaining the underdeveloped world as a safe place for our own economic expansion, it would have been fine if we could have proved in Vietnam that the bravest guerrilla warriors could not succeed, but the contrary has been demonstrated. No people that feels put upon by a great power, or is desperate from deprivation, will ever forget what the Vietnamese people have done against odds that seemed to be absolutely overwhelming.

Likewise, our goal of gaining one more outpost in Southeast Asia for the containment of China and Communism has backfired. As *The Wall Street Journal* put it, "the Communists are getting away with it; they are putting the mighty U.S. through a wringer, and they may be encouraged to try more of it."

This is because our leaders blindly failed to put themselves in the shoes of their opponents. It never seems to have occurred to them that the domino doctrine could work both ways. Accordingly, they confidently attacked North Vietnam, thereby outraging Communists of every known variety, and they were all expected to stand by while we coerced North Vietnam endlessly, year after year, as much as we felt necessary. Though China had thrown us back from her Korean border only a few years ago, she was expected to acquiesce in anything we did to North Vietnam.

When China and Russia and Eastern Europe did feel obliged to aid North Vietnam, we relied on them not to help her enough to defeat our therapeutic assaults on her. We trusted them all to be wise and mature enough not to fear that if they let us get away with the coercion of North Vietnam one of them would be next. Dominoes was a strictly American game. Nobody else would play it.

Yet the Communist governments and peoples did play it. At every stage they have given Hanoi what was needed to maintain and increase her resistance. Gradually the North Vietnamese were trained to use larger and larger weapons. These were supplied, and before Washington began deescalation at the end of March 1968, Hanoi was reportedly assured of longer-range rockets and nuclear weapons, if we should begin nuclear war, as was strongly hinted.

Of course all of this aid was very small indeed when compared to the air and sea fleets which continually poured every kind of American munitions into South Vietnam, but it was sufficient to bring us to the point of disaster. Moreover, in early 1968 Laos was infiltrated by North Vietnamese troops, from end to end, and Chinese troops were reported to be coming into Cambodia and Thailand. North Korea was keyed for an effort to unify Korea by force, one which we would have great difficulty in countering, especially if the attempt were supported by China and/or Russia. The reverse dominoes were poised for falling against us, even at Berlin, where the restrictions on travel were tightened.

The Dominoes of Rejection

The orthodox domino theory worked in reverse, under the constant thunder of our bombing of North Vietnam, but it worked also in equally ominous ways not anticipated by our leaders.

For years the dominoes of disapproval of our actions clattered away from Vietnam throughout Asia, by the hundred millions. They fell also throughout the underdeveloped world, as even the most illiterate people watched the unending spectacle of the big white man constantly belaboring the small colored man, and as the educated contemplated the calamity of being saved from social revolution by American destruction.

Worse still, the dominoes of rejection have fallen against us throughout the whole of Europe, East and West. Our best friends and kinsmen have been so horrified by what we were doing that no government in West Europe dared to make any move to help us in Vietnam, even if it had wished to do so. The youth of Europe, as I found on a visit last summer, are deeply hurt by the cutting disillusionment of what they see us doing, and they will not soon forgive us. Even the youth of the Soviet Union say: "We did not believe the things our government said about you, but now we know they were true."

The dominoes of disapproval have crashed all around the world, across land and sea. Instead of defending our prestige our leaders have accomplished the opposite. It cannot be remembered too often that *doing what is wrong destroys prestige and doing what is right creates it.* Science and invention have made all mankind one family and nothing, short of the final blasts of fire, can undo the ability of all men to judge what we do. Nothing, either, could stir the wrath of the world more quickly than for us to resort again to the use of atomic weapons against Asians.

It is already time for us to realize, incredible as it is, that the great majority of the people would already have reason in our recent conduct for combining against us. In *The New York Times* for February 20, 1968, Professor Thomas H. Greer, co-author of the official seven-volume *Army Air Forces of World War II*, asked the question: "Is it any wonder that millions of people abroad are beginning to view our nation as a monster to be stopped?"

The question is paralyzing, but it should galvanize us into action to reverse the monster image we are building up.

The Dominoes of Despair

All the while, too, another kind of deadly domino has been falling against us. The tragedy in Vietnam has divided our people as they have not been in a century and it has throttled down the Great Society which had given hope to the one-quarter of us who live in urban or rural slums. In the cities the demands of Vietnam have all but killed hope in the great ghettos which harbor the Negro-Americans, not only by drawing funds away from rehabilitation but taking attention away from the dying centers of our cities, until the tragic death of Doctor Martin Luther King, Jr. and its violent aftermath forced us to see again this mortal threat to our entire future.

A great federal commission had already warned that growing civil war at home might come with each summer. To really eliminate the ghettos would require sums that we have not even imagined yet—*trillions* of dollars, says Gunnar Myrdal—and a vast mobilization of national energies, imagination and good will, all drained away to the fruitless Vietnam struggle.

Before President Johnson's historic decision to de-escalate in Vietnam and retire from the presidential race the prospect was that the dominoes of despair would continue to fall in many millions of American hearts and that we would choose to bomb and blast our own cities "to save them." This is the deadly nemesis which grows directly out of the doctrine that our government has the right to use any weapon to enforce its will upon trouble-some people abroad.

The Fall of Lyndon Johnson

The fruits of this belief were registered in the President's address on March 31, 1968, in which he became the greatest of the falling dominoes in reverse, making decisions that would have been utterly inconceivable in early 1965.

Gone was the proud day of April 7, 1965, when he proclaimed that "We will not be defeated. We will use our power with wisdom and restraint. But we will use it!" He *had* used it, and he had been defeated—by the tenacity of the Vietnamese, South and North, and finally by their stunning Têt offensive early in 1968; by steadily rising world opposition; by constantly deepening division at home; by the disintegration of our world position financially, powered by mounting Vietnam deficits piled on top of never-ending Cold War ones; and finally by the looming evidence that he would be defeated for reelection, either in the Democratic National Convention or in November.

So a haggard President announced a suspension of the bombing of most of North Vietnam—that bombing he had begun with such total confidence on February 7, 1965—and the cessation of which the world had demanded with rising insistence ever since. Three years of escalation having palpably failed, he began deescalation: claiming that the Têt offensive had not really succeeded; calling on the Soviet Union, Britain and Ho Chi Minh to help him get peace; pleading with the Congress to raise taxes to help stop the world run on the dollar; admitting that "there is divisiveness among us all tonight"; and declaring that "I shall not seek and will not accept" nomination for another term as President.

It was clear that he still hoped to save the client state which we have created in South Vietnam. The glaring omission of any mention of the National Liberation Front, which governs most of South Vietnam, and other parts of the address betrayed that, but his offer to go back to "the Geneva accords of 1954, under political conditions that permit the South Vietnamese—all the South Vietnamese—to chart their course free of any outside domination or interference, from us or from anyone else," opened the door to genuine self-determination by the South Vietnamese, at last.

Needless to say, our opponents in Vietnam would never agree to an election managed by the current regime in Saigon. They could not countenance that sink of corruption or deal with the group of military officers who have fought with the foreign invaders, both French and American.

This means the continuance of hostilities until our Saigon facade disintegrates or until we remove it and help create an acceptable transitional government. After that some mutually acceptable plan will have to be worked out to insure the freest elections possible.

The Future

In the weeks since March 31, 1968, we have engaged in bombing of unprecedented destructiveness in the lower part of North Vietnam, where the lines of communication run south, as deadlock in the negotiations with Hanoi persists in Paris over its demand for abandonment of the bombing. In this same period, too, the bitter loss of Senator Robert F. Kennedy by assassination has restored the prospect that we shall again have to choose in November between two men who cannot be trusted to make peace—between Nixon the tough hawk and Humphrey the unstable one. This would again drive great numbers of our young people, and others, into despair of our democratic system.

Yet if we are determined enough, the will of the American people to stop trying to police the world can be made known to any president. Using many new means of pressure, we did topple the proud, determined Johnson and our will can be made effective through a lesser reflection of either Goldwater or Johnson. A large segment of our people is deeply stirred by what has happened, ready to react strongly and promptly to any new attempt to crack down forcibly on social dissenters, abroad or at home. They can make themselves heard again.

For the present the essential is a clear understanding of the principles of making peace in the Far East. In addition to a bona fide self-determination for all the people of South Vietnam, these include the sane proposals of majority leader Senator Mike Mansfield for peace with China in his recent lecture at the University of Montana. He rightly stressed that the new China has come to stay; that Taiwan is a part of it and must be so regarded; that Peking has not demonstrated any eagerness to use force against its neighbors, even in the case of India; and that "there is an immense potential danger in China, but there is also an immense potential danger in every other powerful nation in the world which has not yet learned to maintain civilized survival in a nuclear age, except at the razor's edge."

With every prospect of the present nuclear China soon becoming armed with "a full-fledged intercontinental ballistic missile force," Mansfield does not see any reassurance in our giant and tremendously costly armed encirclement of China, all the way from South Korea around to Thailand. To escape from this perfect prescription for world disaster, he urges that we make it "crystal clear that this government does not anticipate, much less does it seek, the overthrow of the government of the Chinese mainland," that we abandon our effort to apply a trade blockade to China, that we evince our readiness to restore travel mutually between us, and that we make it "unequivocal that we are prepared at all times to meet with Chinese representatives—formally or informally— in order to consider differences between China and the United States over Vietnam or any other question of common concern." He urges us to look at China "not through the fog of an old and stagnant hostility, but in the light of enduring interests of the United States in the Western Pacific."

This is a mature view of what is necessary for us to live as a neighbor of the Chinese quarter of humanity in the nuclear age. It is doubtful that either Humphrey or Nixon is mature enough to grasp and act on this necessity, but the one who is our next president must be educated to the extreme urgency of returning to the good neighbor policy in our relations with the world. Nothing less will turn our national energies away from killing the American Dream in the hearts of all foreigners and toward saving it here, where it is also desperately imperiled.

If we will really make the American way valid at home, the peoples will look to us with respect again, not because of the devastating power of our great military-industrial complex, with its vast economically sterile expenditures, but because of what we are.

7

What Are Our Responsibilities in Asia?

1968

Our urge to have profitable dealings with Asia is very deep. It led Columbus to discover America and our colonial forefathers to send the famous clipper sailing ships to China. It led John Quincy Adams, who acquired our first foothold on the Pacific in 1819, to celebrate the event as his greatest achievement and William Henry Seward to call the Pacific "the chief theater of events in the world's great hereafter," well before he obtained Alaska for us in 1869.[1]

Walter LaFeber has shown that as early as 1778 a South Carolina historian thought we had laid the foundations of a new empire, which ever moved from east to

[1] Walter LaFeber, "The Conquest of History: America's Long Dream in Asia," *The Nation*, November 6, 1967, pp. 456–459.

west, and would enable us to have "our turn to figure on the face of the earth and in the annals of the world." He finds, too, that the long, twenty-five year depression in our industrial centers which began in 1873 led succeeding administrations after 1893 to prefer joining in the struggle for Asian markets to reform of the economy. The annexation of the Philippines in 1898, over the armed resistance of the Filipinos, was a part of this process.[2]

This event came during a long, sustained drive by our churches to Christianize China. Legions of missionaries were sent to save the souls of the Chinese, who often regarded them as a part of the process of Western invasion and control, which lasted more than a century and was only ended by the coming of the Communists to power after World War II.

The vast Chinese cultural and political area, which had demonstrated remarkable continuity for thousands of years, had been subjected to every kind of attack, invasion, occupation and humiliation by the Europeans, who too often treated the natives as dirt. This would have festered long in the soul of any people, but the injury was deepened by the fact that China had immemorially considered herself the center of the universe, beyond which all was barbaric and inferior. John King Fairbank has explained vividly how modernization was an exhilarating process for us—always expanding, conquering and prevailing—but it *destroyed* the old China and degraded her people in the process. He is sure that when

[2] *Ibid.* See also his book, *The New Empire.*

Mao speaks of imperialism he thinks mainly of the Western invasions.[3]

Mao cannot forget how the Westerners forced their way into the celestial kingdom, waged wars to enforce subservience, built great alien cities in China's ports, policed her rivers with their gunboats, collected her customs duties and broke down an ancient, viable way of life. Above all, a great and tenacious culture was violated. It does not help us in Chinese minds, either, that we Americans used little force upon China, leaving that to others while under the Open Door doctrine we successfully insisted on obtaining all privileges in China which had been extorted by others.

On our side we are aggrieved that our great missionary effort in China has been so largely negated, and that the great ally across the Pacific which we so wholeheartedly sought to establish after World War II should suddenly became Communist and hostile. We do not understand that Communist China is the real reply to the century of China's trampling by the West, and we greatly resent that this upstart regime forced us to accept a stalemate in the Korean War.

This is one of the main reasons for our clinging to and expanding the close military encirclement of China, which in turn infuriates patriotic Chinese and convinces them that America is their main and implacable enemy, though the current Maoists appear to regard the Soviet Union as their chief foe.

[3] John King Fairbank, *China: The People's Middle Kingdom and the U.S.A.* (Cambridge, Mass.: Harvard University Press, 1967), pp. 98 ff.

The result of the Maoist mentality is an angry, dissatisfied China which feels herself encircled by hostile powers. Moreover, she feels isolated by the failure of her efforts to stir revolts in Africa or elsewhere and by the smashing of the large, friendly Indonesian Communist Party after the coup attempt in October 1965. However, it does not follow that a sullen Red dragon is about to thrash all of its neighbors with its giant tail.

There is no reason to doubt that the new China does intend to try to restore China's ancient cultural and political hegemony in East Asia, as far as she can. Her main aim appears to be to recover suzerainty over Outer Mongolia and adjoining parts of the Soviet Union. Elsewhere she does seek definite boundaries and détentes, her general goal being "a Sinocentric, Asian-oriented power system." [4]

Hans J. Morgenthau agrees that China's aim is to restore her pre-colonial status as an Asian Great Power. If she consolidates her power, she could go much further, but she "has never done so in the past and is not likely to do so in the future." Like the Soviet Union, she is discovering that the risks of promoting world revolution are "out of all proportion to the chances of achieving that revolution." He finds Lin Piao's famous manifesto of

[4] These are the judgments of Norman Ginsberg. See his "On the Chinese Perception of a World Order" in *China in Crisis*, Vol. II, pp. 83–88, edited by Tang Tsou after a series of conferences and papers about China at the University of Chicago. An excellent collection of studies, published by the University of Chicago Press, 1968. Vol. I, in two books, deals with China's Heritage and the Communist Political System.

September 1965, urging the rural peoples of the world to rise up and overwhelm the industrialized countries, to be "intellectually absurd and politically impractical." If China gets a rational government they will "adapt their policies to the real world." [5] He stresses that the issue posed by China is "political and cultural predominance," not military, which cannot be contained by arms, and Donald Zagoria agrees that few students of China would say that she "regards direct military expansion as a major instrument of foreign policy. . . . Indeed any careful study of Chinese foreign policy during the past 15 years would have to conclude that China's main concern has been defensive." [6]

Nor can China hope to solve her desperate population problem by regaining desert or semi-arid lands to the north by fighting the Soviet Union, or by seizing the rice regions of Vietnam. Her billion people, soon to be, can survive only by drastic birth control, rapid industrialization, more scientific agriculture, world trade and perhaps some limited aid from friendly peoples. Conquest of small neighbors at the risk of a great war would be a futile palliative which the highly intelligent Chinese are not likely to attempt—unless they should finally feel suffocated by a strangling containment from the United States and/or the Soviet Union.

[5] *China in Crisis*, pp. 93–95. None of the Chicago experts took any stock in our government's claim that the Lin Piao address was another *Mein Kampf*. On the contrary, it exhorted the underdeveloped lands to revolt but not to look for any outside aid. This is why his address was never published in Hanoi, but otherwise refuted there.
[6] *Ibid.*, pp. 250–253.

Therefore it would seem to be imperative common sense for us to begin to relax, gradually but steadily, our close encirclement of China, along with our total trade embargo. This hostile embrace was originally due to the accident of World War II leaving us in control of South Korea, Japan, Okinawa, and Formosa. Now we have completed the iron ring by seizing South Vietnam and arming Thailand heavily.

How much of this giant "containment" can be said to be in our national interest, in view of China's real weakness as a great power and of her most urgent need to straighten out her domestic politics and cope with immense internal problems? She is not likely to settle down for the long pull at home until after Mao's passing, when his dream of keeping his revolution rolling into the future will have to yield to the inexorable force of evolution, much of it in conservative directions. But after our terrible catharsis in Vietnam there is no need for us to wait for a China that we can love again before we begin to disengage from our overcommitment in Asia. Johnson's dreams of defending us in Asia, along with power and profit there, should go with him.

In a very thoughtful and prophetic article in the *Yale Review* (Winter, 1969), Professor Lawrence Battistini, of Michigan State University, noted that "we have taken over the role of dominator of Asia," seeking in every way "to transform China into the pariah of the international community." He warned that "we are interfering with the natural reordering of Asian international relationships," involving the rise of China to the dignity of a power of the first rank, and that "there is not going to be any real peace in Asia until the Asian dust kicked up by the defeat of imperialist Japan and the post-Second World War revolutions settles in its own way, without a power eight to ten thousand miles away trying to regulate and control its fall."

Our Obligations in Asia

What are our legitimate interests and obligations in Asia?

South Korea

South Korea may be our least soluble problem. We have already suffered severe losses and humiliations there. The southern half of Korea is poor in resources and rich in swelling population, due to reach three hundred million in a century. Until a few years ago there seemed no future for it except a union with the North, but lately a combination of continued massive American aid and Japanese economic reentry—plus considerable authoritarian rule—has produced a minor "economic miracle." Desperate urgency has gone out of the problem, from our standpoint. However, the burden of keeping two heavy divisions of our troops on the firing line in the north and of supporting six hundred thousand native troops remains, in addition to the ever present danger that another Korean War may break out.

It is not certain that a majority of the South Koreans have reconciled themselves to permanent disunity, but there is no doubt that the regime in the North has not, and the aging Kim Il-sung appears to have set reunification as the supreme goal of his life. His commandos almost reached the palace in Seoul lately, to kill President Park, and they are landing far south of the capital in an effort to start guerrilla enclaves.

At the moment, China is too weak to back them in another war and certainly too cautious. Nor does Russia wish another conflict there. But if war breaks out a few years hence, perhaps in a time of high tension with the United States over Berlin or Cairo, and when China is stronger? Are we to carry forever the financial drain of maintaining the division of Korea? Is it really our mission to control the thumbs of Asia permanently, and to keep small nations divided? With Japan strong and rearmed again, some years hence, will it be vital to us to protect her from the Korean "dagger"?

These are questions we should be thinking about before the lack of answers to them lands us in another major bloodletting in Asia, entailing another near bankruptcy and peril of civil war at home. Considering Korea's location, it could not be wise to assume that our position there is permanently tenable and supportable, especially when a very long history is considered.

In "America and East Asia: A New Thirty Years War?" Richard Harris, the Far Eastern specialist of the London *Times*, comes to "the conclusion that American purposes in the East Asian context are unlikely to be achieved." In China, North Vietnam, and North Korea there are governments in power which claim to be "the only righteous government of the country, backing this claim by the accepted and traditional attitude to doctrine." And, he continues, these three governments "seek to unify the country as a whole out of both nationalist and Communist conviction" and, in each case, "it is the anti-Communist side, backed by the Americans, that refuses to allow any contact between the anti-Communist and Communist parts that might lead to reunification."

Harris stresses that the three divided countries "are all part of one civilization. And the problem that America faces within this civilization is different in kind from what America faces in any other of her anti-Communist causes elsewhere in the world." He asks whether "a government in South Korea, lacking any doctrine but anti-Communism, will be able to win the loyalties of Koreans merely by economic success."

He is convinced that we must extricate ourselves from Vietnam and that "some time disengagement will have to follow in Formosa and in South Korea, though the timing and the solution will be different in each case." [7]

---

[7] Published by *The Times*, 1968. See especially pp. 45-64.

After analyzing the deep currents of culture, religion and racial intermingling in the history of South Vietnam, Harris concludes that we "could hardly have chosen worse grounds than South Vietnam to stand on politically." Stressing again that East Asian civilization is different from the rest of Asia, he is sure that "democracy runs against all East Asian traditions and will not be implanted by outsiders," whereas "East Asian Communism is adapted to East Asian needs and becomes thereby inherently unexportable. The renewal of its own civilization is China's prime purpose. The Chinese have rarely been successful im-

His most disquieting observation is that the decisions of our leaders to control South Vietnam were taken by men "almost wholly ignorant of the civilization into which they were intruding."

They thought they had the "power" to do this, from Dulles to Johnson, without realizing that there are powers of the spirit that exceed those of the laboratories of death, and strengths in an ancient civilization that excel those of brasher and more brittle newer ones.

These demonstrated truths may perhaps enable us in time to contribute to a peaceful settlement of the Korean problem. There is no reason to believe that either of the two existing governments would accept federation under any terms acceptable to the other, yet the passage of time is likely only to increase the differences to be reconciled.

On April 27, 1969, *The New York Times* published a dispatch from Harrison Salisbury in Seoul, South Korea, saying that "It is a virtually universal conviction in Seoul that, left to themselves, North and South Koreans would plunge again into civil war at the drop of a hat. . . . No South Korean, from top leader to man in the street, believes peace can ever come to Korea . . . without a new and fateful civil war."

This is the result of the decision of our occupation forces in September 1945 not to tolerate a viable and broadly representative government in Korea, already or-

---

perialists. Theirs is not an outgoing civilization, but rather an *indrawing* one." In others parts of Asia an impulse toward democracy does exist. (Pp. 58–64.)

ganized to govern all of it. Now, after one terribly bloody
civil war there, is it beyond our wit to devise a solution
that would ward off a still worse struggle? Such a conflict
could well give us another disastrous push toward world
bankruptcy and into internal disintegration.

We might at least work for the renewal of intercourse
between the divided halves of Korea and for gradual
steps toward unification.

Japan

Coming to Japan, we undoubtedly have an obligation
to defend her against attack, since we disarmed her and
assumed full responsibility for her after World War II.
Yet there seems to be no real fear of attack by China
in Japan, or even of nuclear blackmail. The Japanese
know that the Chinese nuclear bombs are not aimed at
them. Many in Japan are disquieted and dismayed by
the turmoil in China, but they do not regard it as the
prelude to aggression.

On the other hand, Japan, strongly dynamic again
and enjoying the greatest of the postwar economic mir-
acles, is ready to assume a leadership role in Asia. After
making a trip all the way around the eastern and southern rim of China, Drew Middleton of *The New York
Times* was most strongly conscious of the Japanese up-
surge. He was deeply impressed by "the absolute cer-
tainty with which they talked of their futures," by their
"restless dynamism," and by the fact that "a country
literally bursting with energy lies next to a great, largely
underdeveloped continental land mass." He was dis-

quieted by the resurrection of the old Zaibatsu, the great economic combines which powered Japan's thrust into Asia before 1941, and he might have added that the Japanese have resolutely and tenaciously kept our corporations from taking over Japan's economy, as they are doing in so many other countries. This has been a recurrent American complaint for many years.

Now as a power base, home controlled, "the Japanese economy dwarfs that of more pretentious countries like France," and he is sure "that when and if Japan begins to exert leadership in Asia it will be no more acceptable to Washington than France's attempts to do the same in Europe." Also he found "open lively discussion in Japan of recourse at some future date to nuclear weapons." [8]

It does not seem likely, therefore, that we shall be required to protect Japan. The much greater prospect is that she will become a power in Asia, not necessarily another militaristic one, and a rival, rather than a long acquiescent ward. It is a legitimate endeavor on our part to try to keep Japan in the West, out of fear that the world balance would be tipped against us dangerously if the world's third industrial power joined an Eastern

[8] Drew Middleton, *America's Stake in Asia* (Philadelphia: Lippincott, 1968), pp. 22–41. The theme of the book is the struggle of the small states of Southeast Asia to remain independent against pressures of every kind from Communist China. Nearly all the people he talked with feared the future, first because of North Vietnamese "aggression" and secondly because of the threat of Communism, personified by China. The area is very rich and already "the scene of a great joint effort between Americans and Asians." We are already in Asia and "What we do there will decide the future of that continent in this century." (Pp. 1–20, 198–232.)

combination. But Japan is well Westernized and more likely to prefer to have a foot planted in both worlds, or rather a role as a strong power in between them.

This probability conflicts with the indefinite use of Japan by the United States as a military base, and this includes Okinawa, lynch pin of our chain of containment but strongly rebellious against our presence. On Okinawa there is adamant opposition to the storage of our nuclear weapons there and in Japan 92.6 per cent of the people around our naval bases oppose the visits of our nuclear submarines. Approximately 82 per cent of the people living around U.S. facilities in Japan are against them. Many Japanese who do not oppose the Security Pact do object strongly to the hazards and nuisances created by the bases.

This natural aversion is reported by a seasoned reporter in Japan, Albert Axelbank, in a very significant article, "Short Fuse in Japan." [9] He finds that the Japanese police and military are training and girding for civil war in 1970, when the Security Pact with the United States comes up for review. He predicts that if we cling to our current policies of refusing to heed mass movements in Asia and cracking the skulls of dissenters, we will "foster yet another tragedy in twentieth-century Japan and, as a result, produce irreversible disaster for the American position in Asia," for, without a firm alliance with Japan "the effectiveness of U.S. military power in Asia is slashed at least in half. This dooms American supremacy in Asia."

Another specialist on our relations with Asia, Jeffrey P.

[9] *The Nation*, February 3, 1969.

Freed of San Francisco State College, reporting from Japan to *The Nation* on March 5, 1969, found a formidable list of grievances against our presence piling up: resentment against the prostitution of their women around our bases; fear of constantly recurring U.S. military air accidents and of the transportation of our jet fuel and ammunition on trains and highways; noise from our jet planes; strong opposition to the visits of our nuclear powered ships, especially in fishing waters; and fear of involvement in our wars through the U.S.-Japan Security Treaty. Freed predicted that failure to revise or abolish this treaty soon "can lead only to a broadening of anti-Americanism in Japan, and an increase in violent anti-government activity in the 1970's which will make the demonstrations of the 1960's seem pale in comparison."

One should hardly need add that our indirect control, through Chiang Kai-shek, of Quemoy and Matsu, islands near or in Chinese harbors, is manifestly temporary. No large, proud nation would suffer this indignity any longer than it could do something about it, and it is a central weakness of our close peripheral containment ring that we cannot prevent the growth of local Chinese military superiority. It will also be better for all concerned if these untenable outposts of Formosa are returned to China without an armed conflict that could spread dangerously.

Taiwan

This brings us to the insoluble nexus of our confrontation with China. We are pledged by treaty, honor and other interests to defend the regime of Chiang Kai-shek from destruction by China, and no Chinese government will surrender its claim to recover the island.

Nevertheless, I have come to believe that Taiwan need not be the flash point for an inevitable U.S.-China war. The turmoil in China has postponed notably the time when China may be expected to have a nuclear arsenal strong enough to enable her to defy the United States by attacking Taiwan. Until lately it was reasonable to expect such a moment as perhaps fifteen years away. Now, twenty-five years or longer is more likely.

Therefore, there appears to be time in which to work out a Taiwan solution that, in the end, all parties could or might accept. In *China in Crisis* Robert Scalapino, of the University of California, examined the possible ways out of continuing to support the fiction that Chiang's regime on Taiwan is China. Considering the advantages of recognizing Chinese sovereignty over Taiwan—that Chinese nationalism would not be defied, that the issue of ousting Chiang's Republic of China from the United Nations could be postponed and the way left open for a reconciliation with China—he still concluded that we should declare for an independent Taiwan. This would promote the interests of the people of Taiwan, of non-Asians in general, and would therefore be in our national interest. The Taiwanese would be spared the drastic drop in their standard of living and the severities that would accompany Communist rule from China, things we could not permit to happen. The independence of the island is a fact and the Taiwanization of its government inescapable, a process rapidly becoming a fact as the aging mainlanders pass from the scene.[10]

Chiang's surviving group would bitterly reject our recognition of Taiwan's independence, since they have long misgoverned the island as merely one of the thirty-five provinces of China and accorded it a small voice in the Taipei government only on that basis. China would also be affronted, since she agrees that Taiwan is an inalienable bit of China. But the right of the islanders to self-government in the relatively near future would be assured, after more than fifty years of separation from China and after the nightmare of Chiang's rule which began with "the commission of large-scale genocide against the Taiwanese upper classes in 1947."

In addition to the great gain of self-determination for the islanders, Richard A. Falk, of Princeton University, points out that the present situation inflicts on the United Nations the absurdity of having an unpopular government on an island serve as the only permanent member of the Security Council for Asia. We need to repudiate the claims of the dwindling mainland elite in Taipei to be China and to withdraw support of claims by Taipei to represent China in all international organizations. We can still maintain nonrecognition of China, Falk continues, and our commitment to protect Taiwan from attack would rest on firmer legal and moral grounds. Debate in the United States and the United Nations

[10] *China in Crisis*, Vol. II, pp. 109–120.

could also be shifted to more realistic and legitimate issues.[11]

This reasoning is persuasive. We need greatly to break out of the farcical pose of defending the Taiwan regime as the legitimate government of China, and this can be done with little risk of precipitating an armed conflict in the Formosa Strait. For a couple of decades at least there is small prospect that China could invade Taiwan, even if our armed forces stood aside. Given the plenitude of arms and the training that we furnish Taiwan, China has little prospect of having either an air force or a navy that could take control of the one hundred miles of water in the Strait.[12] Given a few decades, too, both the Chiang and Mao regimes will be gone and the Taiwan issue should progressively lose its irreconcilable character.

Our relations with China must be moved out of hostile deadlock, especially at the point of deepest opposition. Even from the balance of power viewpoint it would be well to have this process begun before the passing of Mao, since his opponents, both civilian and military, favor cooperation with the Soviet Union to industrialize China—"construction before destruction."

Vietnam

But, if it be granted that a normalization in the Formosa Strait is in everyone's best interest, must we not cling to the southern bastion of the containment ring, South Vietnam? The two immense military bases at

[11] *Ibid.*, pp. 127–134.
[12] Brigadier General Samuel B. Griffith II, *Ibid.*, p. 198.

Danang and Camranh that we have built in South Vietnam, plus another in Thailand—each at the cost of a couple of billion dollars—make no sense even theoretically unless they are to restrain the southward pressures of the dragon.

From John Foster Dulles to the end of Dean Rusk's term there has always been an American determination to keep both Communism and China out of South Vietnam and to maintain it in friendly hands as the strategic key to Southeast Asia and beyond. Mr. Rusk's fixation on this point is well known. From his allegation in a speech in May 1951 that the "Peiping" regime might be a colonial Russian government but it was "not the government of China," he has been an adamant opponent of the new China.[13] On October 12, 1967 he bluntly termed the Vietnamese war a testing ground for Asia's ability to withstand the long-term threat of "a billion Chinese armed with nuclear weapons." On January 11, 1968, when asked at the Commonwealth Club in San Francisco: "What are our vital interests in Asia?" he replied that "an unlimited appetite running free in Asia would jeopardize our vital interests." When asked if a united Vietnam would not be a better bulwark against this peril, he replied that we were "defending small nations against world revolution and wars of 'national liberation.' "[14]

Yet others of our leaders have had difficulty in making up their minds about what we were fighting for in Viet-

[13] Neal D. Houghton, *Struggle Against History* (New York: Washington Square Press, 1968), p. 332.
[14] *San Francisco Chronicle*, October 13, 1967; San Francisco television, January 11, 1968.

nam. Theodore Draper has detailed their ambivalence. "First, North Vietnam was substituted for the Southern-based Viet Cong as the 'real enemy.' Then Communist China was substituted for North Vietnam." The "official American line insisted endlessly on the Chinese menace in Vietnam and the North Vietnamese subservience to the Chinese Communists," even after the Soviet Union had become by far the greatest supplier of the sinews of war to North Vietnam. The "American reaction to the increasing Soviet sponsorship of Vietnam was well beyond the permissible limits of self-deception." There came to be "something hallucinatory about the theory that Communist China is the real enemy in Vietnam or that the Vietnamese war is but the preliminary stage of a showdown with China."

In his book, *Responsibility and Response*, General Maxwell Taylor, who had so much to do with our tragic entanglement in Vietnam, could not make up his mind where the real trouble centered. On page 26 he insisted that "it was perfectly clear that the direction, the reinforcements, and the leadership came from the North." That was the "real source" of the guerrilla strength. Yet on page 38 he wrote that if "everything of value in the North were destroyed, we would still have over 200,000 armed guerrillas in the South" who could live off the land and "conceivably remain in action for the next ten, or the next twenty years, and we might be tied down by this vast guerrilla force." [15]

[15] Theodore Draper, *Abuse of Power* (New York: Viking Press, 1967), pp. 127–152.

General Taylor left open the theoretical possibility that this great guerrilla force might have been sent down from the North, fully armed, but the evidence is overwhelming, in a shelf of books about Vietnam, that the United States aborted the provisions of the 1954 Geneva settlement providing for a single Vietnam and set up a tyrant in Ngo Dinh Diem, who created a great rebellion in the South by his efforts to impose his rule on an unwilling people. In their exhaustively documented history of *The United States in Vietnam*, George McT. Kahin and John W. Lewis show that the United States promoted and assisted the flight of nine hundred thousand Catholic elite, who had served the French, from North Vietnam, at a cost of nearly $100 million, and made them the basis of the Saigon regime which still rules a largely Taoist and Buddhist majority.[16]

Their long account of the origins of the civil war demonstrates that far from creating the National Liberation Front (NLF) in the South, Hanoi attacked its broadcasts consistently for months after they began in mid-1958. By March 1960 the veterans of the Vietminh struggle against the French were bitter against Hanoi, calling its emissaries sent to test Southern public opinion cowards. Not until September 5–10, 1960, when it was evident that all influence in the South was at stake, did the

[16] George McTurnan Kahin and John W. Lewis, *The United States in Vietnam: An Analysis in Depth of America's Involvement in Vietnam*, Delta, 1967, pp. 73–76. A table shows a total of $2,397 billion of economic aid to Saigon from 1954 through 1965. Much of this went to the top levels in the form of luxury goods, to create a loyal governing elite.

Communist party of the North sanction the overthrow of Diem. There is "no evidence" for the assertion of the United States "White Paper" of 1965 that the NLF "was formed at Hanoi's order." [17]

Given this background, it is not strange that at this writing, in October 1968, Washington halts the bombing again and gives every evidence of desiring a rapid de-escalation of its commitment in Vietnam. Even Mc-George Bundy, who was a power behind President Johnson when the great escalation began in February 1965, argued on October 13, 1968, for bringing 100,000 to 150,000 troops home from Vietnam in each of the next three years, working into voluntary service for a garrison of about 100,000 men in Vietnam. He offered no regrets for the original campaign of escalation, terming it a decision "to stand and fight in South Vietnam," and he clearly intended to reduce the drain of maintaining a protectorate over South Vietnam to a point the American people would accept.

Hans Morgenthau called the new Bundy plan the "road to disaster on the installment plan at home and abroad" and I. F. Stone observed that this mini-imperialism would still prevent the reforms and reconstruction in the United States which we so desperately need. To Bundy's claim that we must not be accused of "faithless withdrawal" he replied that in its new parliamentary dress the current Saigon regime still represented the 10 per cent pro-war Catholic minority, the landlords, and the North Vietnamese refugee generals "against a South

[17] *Ibid.*, pp. 99–120.

and Central majority *of every class*, which is for some kind of compromise with the Viet Cong." [18]

It must be recognized that our government does have a responsibility not to desert precipitately the small, highly unrepresentative leadership in the Saigon regime, so largely composed of Northern refugees who would like to conquer the North, though from the standpoint of Vietnamese nationalism they are double traitors for having fought first with the French and then with the Americans against their own country. It is still essentially one country in feeling, in spite of all our efforts to cut it into two. Kahin and Lewis come to the central conclusion "that Vietnam is a single nation, not two." [19]

This continues to be the basic reality and it suggests that the Vietnamese will eventually reunite, not only because of the demonstrated power of their nationalism, but because the North and the South strongly need each other economically. In the meantime there can be no peace in Vietnam while we continue to prop up a "government" which is without any effective popular support.

It is clear that we owe its leaders, at the worst, assistance to a comfortable exile, for which most of them are already well provided. The antagonism between them and the NLF appears to be total, and due to our pulverization of Vietnamese society with our big weapons "the NLF, while it has the allegiance of only a minority is still the one cohesive organization in a fragmented society."

[18] *I. F. Stone's Weekly*, October 21, 1968; *The New Republic*, November 2, 1968.
[19] *Supra.*, p. 335.

This is the conclusion of Elizabeth Pond in a long article surveying our future in Vietnam. She accepts the looming probability of "Hanoi's rule of Vietnam and its hegemony of Indochina" but suggests that this can be delayed by gradualness in phasing out our troops from Vietnam, over a period of a few years.[20]

On the other hand, Professor Richard A. Falk, of Princeton University, has found real possibilities for a broader coalition in South Vietnam. After a week of talks with the highest officials in Hanoi and after conferences with NLF officials there and in Paris, he reported his findings in a very significant article in *War/ Peace Report* for November 1968.

Falk is convinced that the new "Alliance of National and Peace Forces" in South Vietnam, outlawed by the Thieu-Ky regime, is an effort by responsible and conservative elements in Saigon and Hue to salvage an independent sovereign South Vietnam, in cooperation with the NLF. In Hanoi he found evidence of a sincere desire, in the ring of voices as well as in what was said, to avoid a purge in South Vietnam. Our opponents insisted that the present Saigon rulers would have to leave the country, though they estimated this group to number "under one hundred." Falk himself expected some reprisals at the

---

[20] Elizabeth Pond, *The Christian Science Monitor*, June 21, 1968. Reports by many impartial newsmen have long indicated that the majority of the NLF leaders "fought the French and now want the Americans out." This has been verified lately by two highly respected leaders of our press, Harry Ashmore and William Baggs in their book *Mission to Hanoi* (New York: Berkeley Publication, 1968)—*Between the Lines*, published by Charles A. Wells, November 15, 1968.

district and local levels. After so much bitterness and hostility, he thought we could hardly hope to get a stable government without some accompanying bloodshed.

He was convinced that the first coalition government would have to be *negotiated* rather than elected and that an attempt to hold an election at once, where there had never been a free one, "might imperil what would otherwise be a mutually acceptable settlement of the war." Elections could be scheduled at a fixed date, perhaps a year later and under the supervision of some neutral observation group.

This is a commonsense conclusion, accompanied as it is by an acceptance of sovereign status for South Vietnam, pending gradual reunification not tied to a timetable. Some fourteen years of enforced separation have created interests and differences in the two halves of the country that will have to be adjusted gradually. Falk was impressed with the cruelty of the sealed border between South and North since 1954. Its reopening to long-divided families and other human needs would both promote unity and remove the urgency for it.

He believed that this normalization of life in Vietnam should be accompanied by a withdrawal of our military forces "rather rapidly," again a reasonable requisite of genuine self-determination. Of course it will be said that this is no way to guarantee our "strategic" and imperial interests in Southeast Asia, but the eagerness of the Vietnamese for a neutralized status and their tragically demmonstrated willingness to fight for their independence, against all comers, should be the best protection for our legitimate interests in the area. Certainly, too, "the daily horror of the war is too great" for us to postpone a settlement.

On our side, Washington has at various times declared publicly that: (1) We want no United States bases in Southeast Asia; (2) We do not desire to retain United States troops in South Vietnam after peace is assured; (3) We support free elections in South Vietnam to give the South Vietnamese a government of their own choice; (4) The question of reunification of Vietnam should be determined by the Vietnamese through their own free decision; and (5) The countries of Southeast Asia can be nonaligned or neutral if that be their option.[21]

These are principles, if fairly applied, under which the Vietnamese could have genuine self-determination. Everything depends on the application. For example, "free elections" if administered by the United Nations, strongly present in Vietnam, would give one result and a manipulated "election" by the current government, under its rules, a very different one. How it works out will determine whether we stand upon the bed rock foundation of democracy, or whether we use a caricature of it to maintain our control of South Vietnam.

There is room for a phasing out of American troops from Vietnam over a reasonable, definite period. There could be a longer American armed presence in Thailand, until the Thais feel strongly that it is a liability, as many already do, involving the corruption of their society at all

[21] *Department of State Bulletin*, Washington, February 14, 1966. Cited in Kahin and Lewis, p. 436.

levels. Proverbially adept in balancing powers that press upon them, they may soon see that the Asian countries that have become outposts of American military power— Laos, South Vietnam, and now Thailand herself—have become magnets for Communist subversion.[22] Their leaders may soon decide that the best defense against Communism is not American military power, but greater efforts to reduce corruption and extend social services to their poorer people.

(In the meantime, Senator George McGovern, one of the most conscientious members of the Senate, gave that body, on March 17, 1969, the detailed evidence that while ostensibly pursuing peace in the negotiations at Paris our Government greatly extended its offensive operations in the South. In the three months after the bombing halt in the North, in October 1968, the number of battalion-size operations on our side in the South climbed from 820 to 1077. Combat operations were being admittedly extended into Laos. Marine units claimed publicly "the largest amphibious operation since the end of World War II," and air bombings by the giant B-52s were greatly extended.

Since "the North Vietnamese had responded to our bombing halt by withdrawing 22 full regiments from South Vietnam," it was not surprising that they resumed the shelling of several dozen towns and American installations nightly for several months. Our casualties also rose to record heights—totalling 12,400 dead and 37,000

[22] Hans Morgenthau, *China in Crisis*, Vol. II, p. 102.

seriously wounded since the peace talks began. Mc-Govern was appalled to see us still committed to saving the corrupt Saigon regime, which had no capacity to save itself. This objective was not worth one more American death, especially while "three million Vietnamese refugees still languish in miserable camps—homeless, neglected, despondent." He found it "intolerable that we should still be pursuing the same tragic course with the same tragic results.")

Thailand, Laos, Malaysia, and Singapore

After his Asian tour Drew Middleton regarded these four countries as "the heart of the problem" of maintaining independent non-Communist governments. In each one he found that the leaders regarded the North Vietnamese as aggressive and China as a great potential danger. One of the ablest of them, Prime Minister Lee K. Yew of Singapore, felt that the ultimate survival of all these little states depended on federation. He proposed a group including Malaysia, Thailand, Cambodia, Burma, the Philippines, Indonesia, and Singapore.[23]

Since they produce similar raw materials, they all need economic and technological assistance, which the United States, Japan, and others could give, especially in the climactic struggle to produce enough food to keep ahead of the population explosion. This is the war of the future, which will submerge the capitalist-Communist struggle

[23] Middleton, *America's Stake in Asia*, pp. 64–69.

and require the best efforts of both systems to enable humanity to continue, much less prosper.[24]

The struggle for economic viability in this area may not be highly profitable for Americans, but it should call out our best endeavors.

Indonesia

Nowhere is this struggle more acute than among the one hundred million Indonesians on their ten thousand islands. Middleton found their economic problems more overwhelming than in any other Asian country. This was the situation following the immense blood bath in which from three hundred thousand to one million Communists or alleged Reds were massacred after the abortive coup of October 1965, in which six top generals were slain and another, General Nastution, arch enemy of President Sukarno, was wounded. However, he escaped and led the army's grim reaction to the crime.

Was it hatched in Peking?

Two students of Indonesian affairs who have examined the evidence extensively say no. David Mozingo believes that "It was in Peking's strongest interests that the political situation existing in Indonesia in late 1965 be preserved rather than endangered by any adventurist action from the Left directed against a much stronger and already apprehensive anti-Communist army leadership." He concludes that "no evidence has appeared suggesting that Peking wanted to undermine Sukarno or that it con-

[24] Neal Houghton, *Struggle Against History*, p. 320. Houghton is the first American scholar to see this.

sidered the situation in Indonesia ripe for a PKI takeover." Ruth T. McVey fully concurs in this conclusion,
adding that "It is hard to see why China would have
chosen to do anything but play out the Sukarno string
for as long as it lasted."

Both agree that a state of acute tension did exist between the army leadership and the PKI, apparently related to Sukarno's age and health, and that the coup
could not have been attempted without the "close cooperation of a considerable number of military officers."
Miss McVey includes the air force, which had long had a
bitter rivalry with the army, among those ready for a coup.

She suspects that the smashed Communist social revolutionary movement may be easier to resurrect "than to
create one from a politically inert base," especially since
the current army rulers "have inherited an economy suffering from grave structural defects as well as misman-
agement, an enormous pool of rural and urban discontent, and an elite which has little to unite it beyond the
determination to hold on to what remains of a rapidly
vanishing wealth." [25]

If we really wish to save Indonesia from Communism,
here is a theater in which heroic measures might succeed.
The expenditure of say $15 billion a year for economic

[25] *China in Crisis*, Vol. II, pp. 333–395, especially 340–343, 379–380,
394. In mid-1969 a new edition of Robert Shaplen's *Time Out of
Hand* (New York: Harper and Row) was published, too late for adequate coverage here. An excellent 175-page section on Indonesia contains strong evidence that Sukarno was behind the 1965 Communist
coup and that, fearing his own death, he pushed it to action pre-
maturely. Several circumstances pointed toward knowledge of the plot
in Peking. (110–114).

and technological aid over a six-year period, approximately half of our appropriations for destruction in Vietnam, might make Indonesia a going concern on our model, always provided that the population could be stabilized.

Such a crusade could also enlist all of our missionary and capitalist zeal, as well as providing an outlet for our surplus goods and capital.

India

Here, too, is an immense outlet for our constructive energies. Middleton found there "a desperate situation" with 520 million people already born and a population of a billion by the year 2000 in sight. Immense was the descriptive word for every problem. There was "The enormous gap between rich and poor in a society supposedly seeking socialism," and "the corruption that extends from the highest level to the office boy who must be bribed to carry a file from one desk to another in a government office." There was "staggering administrative inefficiency" and the overriding problem of food, along with the "almost unbearable burdens in defense expenditure." Yet "India must be supported." Fortunately, too, the United States had already given India $1,300,000 "to buy contraceptives in the United States and distribute them through commercial channels," with more to come.[26]

Here again is a limitless field for our idealism and dedication, along with some profits for business. Here, too, a real crusade is required, if India is to be forestalled

[26] Middleton, *America's Stake in Asia*, pp. 117–121.

from resorting to Communism in desperation. Every kind of aid is urgently required—many millions for birth control, billions annually for economic and technical aid, including some for defense against China; and a great campaign to save India will also provide a large outlet for our own explosive economic system, which demands large new investments and mercantile outlets abroad each year.

In the end it would all be in vain, unless India's population is brought under control and basic internal reforms achieved, but we would at least have the satisfaction of keeping babies and their mothers alive, instead of scientifically destroying them in their villages, as in Vietnam.

Australia

An article on the American military presence in Asia by an Australian scholar surveys all the objections to it and finds them all of very doubtful validity. On every score he finds American power a very stabilizing factor. This, too, accords with the natural feeling of Australians that with the withdrawal of British power they are very far from home and very much alone.[27]

This is a natural feeling for some twenty million Europeans inhabiting a large, sparsely settled continent just under the teeming billions of Asia. They inevitably now look to us as their protector and we must not disappoint them. They are akin to us in almost every vital respect

[27] Owen Harris, "Should the U.S. Withdraw from Asia?" *Foreign Affairs*, October 1968, pp. 15–25. The author teaches at the University of New South Wales.

and, if we must sometimes think in global balance of power terms, they are a valuable, dependable ally. Accordingly, there is ample justification for strong commitments to defend them against military attack. If, too, we must have great bases and garrisons somewhere in the Orient, the Australian continent and islands, together with New Zealand, have plenty of room and presumably a warm welcome for them. There would also be a minimum of provocation of any Asiatic people, along with reasonable proximity to many lesser peoples who might be reassured by their presence and by the occasional sight of American ships and planes.

The Philippines

If it be granted that it is our sacred mission to save Asia from Communism, we have a heavy obligation to bear in the Philippines. We took them from Spain in 1898 and then set them free some twenty years ago. Yet Drew Middleton, who believes in our mission in Asia, saw that it is "all too transparently clear that America failed here," that their condition is worse than states like Thailand or Malaysia. "Bribery, corruption, nepotism, social injustice are rife. A potentially rich country is rapidly disintegrating economically." There are thirty-two million people on the islands today and one hundred million are due by the end of the century, but the Republic already depends on food imports. Yet there is "an almost feudalistic system of land tenure." The big landlords control the Congress (as in Saigon) and they will not spend money on technological improvements.

There is "blatant, ubiquitous corruption throughout the government structure and the police exacerbate economic difficulties." Bribery is "everywhere." People who do no wrong "bribe to be let alone by people who could abuse them." Nepotism and political graft accompany a grossly swollen civil service, which is lazy and inefficient. Along with "the social irresponsibility of the rich" the government loses $100 million a year from technical smuggling and more from pirates, some of whom move in fast motorboats to land and loot shops and homes. Nowhere in nearly thirty years as a correspondent had he seen "corruption as unashamed" or felt as unsafe as in Manila.

It would seem to be a 100 per cent safe understatement to say that we must hasten back to the Philippines to man the ramparts against Communist China. President Marcos was sure of it. "Asia's principal political-military problem," he said, "is to organize and equalize the military force of Red China which is the central factor in Asian politics." Could anything be clearer? During the fifties the Huk rebellion in the Philippine rural areas was very hard to suppress and now, due to "the present poverty, the inequalities of wealth, the absence of social justice, the lawlessness, and the corruption" it is reviving again.[28]

Is it not clear that we must hold ourselves in readiness to go to bomb and napalm the Philippine peasants in

[28] Middleton, *America's Stake in Asia*, pp. 179–190. A special dispatch to *The Province*, Vancouver, B.C. on March 5, 1969, described wholesale smuggling, wars between smugglers and pirates and between pirates, plus revolting crimes in the Philippine-Southeast Asian waters.

their miserable homes? We have taught ourselves that
no possible fate could be worse than Communism. Yet
will we not be obliged to admit eventually that a society
can be so rotten as to be unsavable short of revolutionary surgery? We have a moral obligation to defend the
Philippines against military invasion from China, but
do we have the right or capacity to defend them from
internal revolution?

In his *Time Out of Hand* (see footnote 25) Robert
Shaplen has an illuminating chapter on the Philippines
in which he portrays the dead weight of four-hundred
years of harsh rule by Spanish landlords, and the fitful
but ineffective efforts to end the rule of the "landlord
oligarchy, the dominant force in the country." He was
appalled by "the awful cleavages of wealth and poverty,"
by the failure to "attack corruption from the top down,"
and by the rule of Angeles City, adjacent to our vast
Clark Field, by the Huks, where every kind of racket
flourished. The power of the Huks was so great that
$250 million in American materials was stolen from the
great base each year.

After ten years of visiting the Philippines, Alex Camp-
bell of the *New Republic* staff wrote in its May 24, 1969
issue, from Manila, that middle class intellectuals and
professional people were "thoroughly discouraged and
planning their exodus." Thousands were applying for
visas to the United States.

In general the Philippines were "a smiling cesspool
of hate as far as Americans are concerned," yet they

were really a colony of their own fifty families, who exploited their workers and peasants "more than any foreigners or foreign company would dare do." In these circumstances, our ability to save the Filipinos by destroying them, as in Vietnam, would seem to be limited.[29]

Overriding World Problems

The Population Explosion

We should be ever mindful, too, that similar challenges are boiling up in our own backyard—Latin America, from which we have warned all others away since Monroe proclaimed his Doctrine in 1823. It, too, is our special responsibility and in many Latin lands the same kind of oligarchies, also descended from Spanish rule, monopolize the land and remain impervious to the needs of their peasants, who flee to the cities and live in broad fringes of misery around them.

In Latin America our military power blankets the continent, in the form of weapons, military instruction and

[29] On February 6, 1969, Philippine Foreign Minister Carlos Romulo expressed on NBC television the feeling of his government and others in the far Pacific that they must restudy their policies and alignments. A lecture trip to seventeen American universities, during which he constantly questioned everyone he met, from janitors to university presidents, convinced him that the American people are opposed to any more rescue operations in Asia.

the assurance that the American eagles will fly swiftly to help suppress any serious outbreak of social discontent. But with every hour the population of the region expands at a rate second to none anywhere. In less than thirty years their hungry millions promise to be too many for suppression by our napalm, which has already been tried out in Colombia. The "necessity" to wage other Vietnam wars there would seem imminent, to save these lands from Communism and to save our fast-growing investments throughout the region.

Are we not lost if another country constricts our capitalist expansion room by going Communist? In another ten years the question itself may seem inconsequential. On November 12, 1968, the highly respected author and scientist C. P. Snow delivered a lecture on the subject "The State of Siege" in which he confessed that he had been nearer to despair in 1968 than ever before in his life. Developments in Czechoslovakia, Vietnam and elsewhere had given him "very little reason to hope that the richer countries would ever cooperate with each other enough to head off collision between soaring population and limited food supply, with staggering famine the result." The best information indicated that local famines, visible on our television, would begin in the years 1975–1980 and probably "spread into a sea of hunger." In the meantime, the gap between the rich and poor lands is widening frighteningly. In a large slice of the poor countries, said Snow, the average daily income is about 35 cents as compared with $8 in the United States, twenty times greater. In ten years it is likely to be three hundred times greater. Only concerted efforts by the rich and poor states could save us from being surrounded by the sea of hunger—costing "as much as 20 per cent of the gross national product of the rich countries for ten to fifteen years." [30]

This is the grim magnitude of the real challenge before us. Beside it the issue of capitalism *vs.* communism bids fair to become irrelevant. If either meets the real challenge best, it is likely to prevail; if neither does, they may both disappear; if they combine to deal with the real challenges of the century the difference between them will seem immaterial.

The Destruction of our Environment

Beyond the immediate threat that man will suffocate himself by breeding, even in well-to-do lands, equally deadly threats loom not far behind. Each day man releases into the comparatively thin air jacket of the earth greater quantities of deadly gases and killing smogs. Each day he completes the pollution of lakes and streams, killing all fish life in them. Each day he releases greater quantities of long-lived DDT and other pesticides which finally reach the ocean, where they promise to kill the tiny organisms that replenish our supply of oxygen. If no power-mad or nervous leader presses the red nuclear button, we are still on the way to a fairly early extinction of life on this planet. Scientists warn that a great program

[30] *San Francisco Chronicle*, November 13, 1968.

to halt the deterioration of our environment is of extreme urgency.

Obviously we cannot begin to cope with the deadly perils which confront us all without combining in the United Nations, the World Bank, and other global agencies to wage real war on the practices that can soon destroy us.

The Diversion of Resources to Armaments

Equally obviously we cannot find the resources to succeed in any of the world campaigns that really matter while we continue to squander and sterilize vast amounts of resources in armaments. This, too, appears to be our chosen and dedicated route to extinction. There is "power" and patriotism in it, along with fabulous profits and much employment.

It is perfectly clear, too, that our scientists and those of our cherished rivals are talented enough to pile scientific "weapon systems" on top of each other until some manmade doomsday comes—each one to cost increasing tens of billions of wealth that might help to save humanity. We are told already that stockpiles of the military-industrial complex are sadly depleted by Vietnam and that "defense" expenditures will have to remain on the new high levels. We have also elected a president who wants to make sure that we regain defense superiority, and he has the right Congressional committee chairmen to help him do it.

Concurrently, also, we have conditions of near civil war in our own land of the free, due to the cutting down

of the Great Society programs by the Vietnam War and
the upthrust of a large black minority determined to live
in foul ghettos no longer. They have seen the soaring
affluence around them and want some of it.

The Wasting of Super-Power Leadership

At the same time our reputation as the leader of the
peoples into the future has sunk to near zero. On November 17, 1968, James Reston reported from London that
the effort of Washington, to run the free world looked
like "a bloody awful mess to them." It "would be hard
to overestimate the damage done to American prestige in
this part of the world as a result of the Vietnam War,
and what hope exists here in the election of Nixon rests
in the expectation" that he will end it. But, said the
socialist *New Statesman*, if he cannot deliver, and soon,
"the world of the '70s may make almost any postwar
period look rosily enviable in contrast." On the conservative side, *The Spectator* wrote: "Vietnam matters not
merely for itself. It matters because the U.S. must determine, once and for all, not to allow herself to become
embroiled in any further adventures of this kind. It matters because America's foreign exchange expenditure on
the war, coupled with financial policies that are incom-
patible with this rate of expenditure, threatens to cause
a collapse of the entire international monetary system."
The Economist, clearly worried about the new president
and his constituency, added that his place in history
would probably depend on how successful he is "in sav-

ing his country from the civil war that threatens it." [31]

Nor can we defend ourselves by replying that the British used to have imperialistic troubles. As Hamilton Fish Armstrong, editor of *Foreign Affairs*, has observed, this kind of argument is never effective. "Nor can we make it with any satisfaction to ourselves," he continued. "Too many of us are horrified by the suffering and sorrow we are causing, the wiping out of villages and devastation of cities in South as well as North Vietnam, the relentless recitation of body-counts, the herding hither and yon of pitiful refugees now numbered in the millions. . . ." [32]

"Power in a Sieve"

Power Politics Unplayable

The title of Armstrong's article, "Power in a Sieve," also described our predicament perfectly. Our leaders have been bemused by the "power" they think is put into their hands by our unprecedented military gadgets. All other great powers have always used their power, even in far places, so we must too. Yet to their deep frustration it develops that the power of the spirit in little brown men is even greater, so great as to topple our most powerful leaders from office and threaten the foundations of our national "power."

[31] *San Francisco Chronicle*, November 17, 1968.
[32] Hamilton Fish Armstrong, "Power in a Sieve," *Foreign Affairs*, April 1968, p. 468.

It is still possible to formulate plausible plans and prescriptions for exercising our military power all over the Far East, but after Vietnam who will believe in their efficacy? [33]

With his usual prescience, Walter Lippmann explained in October 1967, before President Johnson admitted that victory in Vietnam had eluded him, why power politics has become unplayable. All of its practitioners were in trouble. Johnson's attempt to use our vast "power" had landed this country in the most serious trouble in a hundred years. De Gaulle, "the most prophetic and experienced of living statesmen, had somehow entangled himself in costly and dangerous miscalculations both in Europe and the Middle East," and in the latter region the Soviet Union had made "a humiliating hash of its opportunities." Britain was in full retreat from empire. The United States had to put up with Castro in Cuba and the Soviets with Israel.

He suggested that the failures of the power players centered in the great technological revolution, "the most radical revolution in the history of mankind," that seems to make our rulers so "powerful." It seems to do so, but at the same time it is changing the lives of people so much and in so many ways—some both bewildering and frightening—that the peoples (in the advanced countries, one might add) are too much absorbed in their own lives to care very much about foreign exploits. And everywhere

[33] See Hanson W. Baldwin, "After Vietnam—What Military Strategy in the Far East?" *The New York Times Magazine*, June 9, 1968, p. 36 ff.

"Nations cannot now be ordered around by coercing or cajoling or bribing their governments." Again one might add because even the poor peoples have finished with imperialism, especially in its cruder forms, and are determined to live their own lives without outside dictation.[34]

A penetrating editorial "Beyond Imperialism" in the *New Republic* for January 27, 1968, marshaled the evidence that the age of imperialism has ended. "The democratic idea of self-determination *has* caught on." The "dream of peace-keeping within and around more primitive societies by an imperial military presence is not dead, as U.S. troops in Vietnam and Thailand illustrate. But it is a dream." [35]

[34] Walter Lippmann, *The Nashville Tennessean,* October 8, 1967.

[35] In a booklet, "East Asia on the Move," issued by the Department of State in 1968, William P. Bundy, Assistant Secretary of State for East Asian and Pacific Affairs, marshalls the economic success stories in Japan, South Korea and Taiwan, along with other evidences that the West still has rising vitality and that our presence is still required in Asia.

He cites the Freedom House statement by fourteen distinguished students of Asia, published in December 1967, attesting that "the basic decision of the United States to maintain a presence in Asia since 1945 has been indispensable to all there who have sought a non-communist route to development and a political equilibrium for the region as a whole."

This should be granted freely. Yet it does not follow that the United States can recover from Vietnam and continue to be responsible for the destinies of all the peoples in the area. Edwin O. Reischauer, one of the fourteen experts, and a recent Ambassador to Japan, does not think that "we really have an Asian policy," and urges that we approach our Asian problems, "not in the haphazard fashion of the past, but with a broad, far look over the terrain ahead of us." (*Look,* April 4, 1967, pp. 21–23.) See also his book, *Beyond Vietnam: The United States and Asia* (New York: Vintage Press, 1968).

George F. Kennan looked in the same direction, saying: "We will be dismayed, I think, to find how much Vietnam has cost us in terms of the confidence and respect of world opinion," and he could see "only one dignified and effective response: withdrawal, abstention, and a dignified silence." It was "little short of fantastic" that we should be pouring a fourth of our budget and half a million of our young men into an area to which our "vital interests are only remotely related." Our reorientation must be "away from the ambitious dreams and extravagant efforts of recent years and in the direction of a new determination and concentration of effort in the ordering of our domestic affairs." [36]

Retrogression in the Soviet Empire

The determination of the smaller peoples to live their own lives is rising also in the Soviet Empire in East Europe, child of World War II which was formed originally for defensive purposes. But exploitation was understandably involved, to enable Russia to recover from her abysmal postwar weakness. Thus the industries of Czechoslovakia were put to work producing heavy goods for Russia and when these were no longer needed, Moscow resented the desire of Prague to reconvert to supply consumers, especially when they looked to the West for machines and credits. The whole Czech economy had stagnated, under frozen bureaucratization, and by 1968 the Czechoslovaks were determined to recover their former democratic liberties, combining them with demo-

[36] *The Christian Science Monitor*, July 5, 1968.

cratic socialism. This is why Novotny, their Stalinist ruler, had to go.

Weeks of agony in Moscow, East Berlin, Warsaw and Budapest, featured by a trip of their top leaders to Slovakia for a conference with the new Czech leaders, finally ended in a sudden massive occupation of Czechoslovakia, with more than half a million troops, many coming by air. No quislings for an old-line government could be found, but by degrees the newly asserted freedoms were curtailed. The hard-liners who prevailed in Moscow could not risk freedom of speech and information.

Only a few people were killed. There were no parallels with Vietnam, except in the essential brutality of the occupation to prevent a small people from determining its own destiny. This great power crackdown, we must believe, will also fail against the aroused determination of the Czechs and Slovaks to live their own lives, without endangering Russia's defense line. There are signs, too, that this same determination is stirring in Russia, not to speak of the many nationalities in the Soviet Union itself.

Toward the Death of all Isms

In spite of the convulsive efforts of great states to conserve or expand their "power," there is a growing oneness of mankind and an irrepressible need everywhere for dignity as well as a fair distribution of the amenities—and necessities—of life. These things are fundamental, as even the giant governments must learn. As a keen observer wrote, Washington tried to save a Novotny-type government in Saigon by bombing North Vietnam. "The result, as the world knows, ripped the fabric of American society, destroyed U.S. prestige and deformed the American economy." And now the Communist hawks may find in Czechoslovakia "their mindless thrust for stability finally to be the most de-stabilizing act of all." [37]

In June 1968 C. L. Sulzberger reported an interview with Milovan Djilas, the Yugoslav dissenter, who said: "We are going toward the death of all isms." He was sure that "all versions of Communism are becoming decadent. They must inevitably change into a democratic society," but one in which "socialism and socialist ownership must be the main force." [38] Of course this is the last kind of democratic society which our own elites desire, but will they not be compelled to adopt more "socialist" reform to preserve the basic structure of our way of life against the revolutionary stresses arising from a third or fourth of our people who are failing to share in the abundance flowing from our explosive economy? In these days of ever faster communications the world is too small for two antithetical, irreconcilable economic and political systems locked in a death struggle. The weaknesses of each of them are too evident and the need to combine

[37] Roy Bennett, ADA World Magazine, November 1968, p. 8 M. In perhaps the last thing he ever wrote, Leo Huberman, an independent American Socialist of high integrity, said: "The hardliners of the Soviet Union and the other invading countries have won only a temporary victory. The end is not yet." (Monthly Review, October 1968, p. 5.)
[38] C. L. Sulzberger, "A Conversation with Yugoslavia's Djilas," The New York Times Magazine, June 9, 1968, p. 30 ff.

their strengths in a world-wide viable way of life is too compelling.

A World Corporate State?

The growth of a world society is being forced by the growth of world corporations, mainly ours, seeking expansion. Our corporate giants constitute the greatest economic force which has ever existed in the world. General Motors alone has annual profits of 20 per cent on its huge investment and gross receipts as great as the gross national product of all but 14 of the 124 nations in the United Nations. The outthrust of the international corporations, says Arthur Barber in a remarkable article, "is rapidly limiting the sovereignty of many nations." Of 1,000 major corporations engaged in foreign operations, 750 are American, with investments of $57.6 billion, and their constant expansion both takes them into scores of countries and forces waves of self-protective mergers in all the advanced countries where they are not excluded. The greater managerial, technological and educational strength of our corporations speeds the process, raising the prospect that "within a generation about 400 to 500 international corporations will own about two-thirds of the fixed assets of the world," presumably the Western world.[39]

Yet in all the Communist countries there is also "a fundamental conflict between the ideologists of the nation state and the technocrats." This conflict appears to

[39] Arthur Barber, "Emerging Power: The World Corporation," War/ Peace Report, October 1968, pp. 3–8.

be universal. To Barber it means that "power is shifting away from the nation state to international institutions, both public and private," such as the Common Market and the International Monetary Fund. There is also a compensatory shift inward—"toward a greater emphasis on domestic problems and on economic growth, rather than fear of and preparation for war."

It would seem clear that the powerful trend toward a world economy collectivized in the hands of a few corporations requires the growth of world political institutions to control them. Inside the American nation state, too, there must be controls over the all-devouring collectivization of our economy which is taking place at an accelerated pace, by some companies swallowing others, at the rate of three thousand conglomerate mergers a year, until one wonders if we may not end before long with a half dozen corporations, or one, owning all the economy that matters. In whose interest then will our economy be administered?

8

Can We Achieve a Workable Role in the World?

1969

The internationalization of much of the world's economic life proceeds, at high speed. The means of military destruction threaten to skyrocket forever. Man moves toward the fatal fouling of his environment at an accelerated pace, and his suffocation by overpopulation is widely and authoritatively predicted. This is the world for which our leaders have assumed primary responsibility, in a globe girdling network of guaranty pacts, and in which the unprecedented outthrust of our economic power proceeds.

In such a world, what guidelines can be laid down for the preservation of a democratic civilization here in the United States, the external operations of which can be accepted by other peoples?

Some Feasible Objectives

Should we not strive for these things?

1. *Challenge our world police mentality.* This is a deep-seated disease. Founded on the Truman Doctrine and apotheosized by Johnson, it has seized a great many powerful Americans. "Somebody has to police the world." Britain used to do it. Now it is up to us. We have the power. Communism must be stopped, and we need the free world for our investments.

Backed by our sad experience in Vietnam it is essential to oppose this dogma and to rise instantly in opposition to any new manifestations of it. This is exactly what happened in the Senate on July 10, 1967, just after President Johnson had sent three planes loaded with troops to support a troubled regime in the Congo. First, Senator Richard B. Russell, chairman of the Armed Services Committee, angrily denounced the move. Then Senators John C. Stennis, J. W. Fulbright, and Mike Mansfield all protested strongly and they were joined by two high Republicans, Milton R. Young and Thruston B. Morton.

This was the top power structure of the Senate, putting its foot down hard at the very first sign of a new Vietnam. These were deeply troubled men who were "coming to believe that the United States is drastically over committed in military and political alliances around the world." The course we are on, said Senator Morton, "started with the Churchill speech in Fulton, Missouri, and we've got to change it." [1]

Faced by this determined front, the Administration rapidly backtracked in the Congo. Naturally, few citizens can make their voices heard against *Pax Americana* so effectively, but every citizen has a Congressman and two Senators, his newspaper letter column and other means of making his voice heard.

2. *Abandon our role as the protector of reaction everywhere.* Nothing could astonish our great leaders, from Washington and Jefferson to Wilson and FDR, more than our current global watch over the welfare of every ruling oligarchy in the world, and our world-wide patrol to protect status quos and repress any popular revolt. Can the nation which has longest asserted and supported the sacred right of revolution really make a success as the world center of counter revolution? Can we abandon a great heritage and reverse completely our role in the world? Can all this be justified in the name of protecting and extending investments? Or is the welfare and survival of the world's peoples the decisive consideration? In the long view of our own self-interest, also, isn't it better to work with the peoples instead of the potentates, many of whom have long overstayed their time?

The leading authority on *Pax Americana* observes that a good many regimes which tell us that we have a responsibility to save them "simply cannot be saved be-

[1] Don Oberdorfer, "Noninterventionism, 1967 Style," *The New York Times Magazine*, September 17, 1967, pp. 28–31, 102–112.

cause they are too corrupt and discredited. Others may not be worth saving." This country "was not meant to be a trustee for regimes in bankruptcy." He adds that "There will be revolution in Latin America, upheaval throughout Asia and the Middle East, and violence in Africa, no matter what we or the Communists do or refrain from doing." [2]

3. *Oppose our anti-Communist obsession with facts.* The main reality of the capitalist-Communist confrontation is still there, and the great advantages and vitality of capitalism are apparent. On the other hand, Communism has set some goals for any good society.

In 1967, on its 50th Anniversary, one of the most competent students of the Soviet Union found the country in "a state of spectacular economic development." The construction of housing has been going on "like mad" for many years and it is now adequate. Moreover, Soviet citizens enjoy three great advantages: (a) extremely low rents; (b) "An absolutely free and highly efficient medical service"; and (c) universal free education which "gives the Soviet people the impression of being perhaps the best-educated, most literate nation in the world, one seized with a genuine passion for education and 'culture,'" many forms of which are cheaply obtainable. [3]

4. *Promote business partnerships with Communist countries.* This may seem insufferable to some capitalist

[2] Ronald Steel, *Pax Americana* (New York: Viking Press, 1967), pp. 331–333.
[3] Alexander Werth, "Year of Jubilee, The USSR at Fifty," *The Nation*, October 30, 1967, pp. 424–430.

ideologues, but it opens a wide field for economic activity. West German firms, led by Krupps, have long been building plants in the Soviet Union and East Europe, the profits to be shared equally with the Communist government concerned. Now French and Italian motor companies are doing the same thing.

Of course this is anathema to the orthodox capitalist, because profits must be shared and because the Red government agency wields the power of control. Yet the arrangement proves that mutually profitable and beneficial business can be done with Communist countries, apart from the wide field of purely commercial transactions.

5. *Work constantly for détente with the Communist powers.* We should seek to normalize relations with China and to bring her into the world community. She may not respond until there are further political changes in China, but all doors should be held open, for she is too large a section of humanity to isolate or "contain."

Indeed, a continued attempt on our part to isolate China could result in our own unintended isolation from her. During February 1969, both Canada and Italy announced their intention to recognize China, which already had diplomatic relations with several NATO countries and many others.

An excellent issue of *The Bulletin of the Atomic Scientists and Public Affairs*, (February 1969), devoted to "China After the Cultural Revolution," contains a warning by Special Editor Dick Wilson that the possibilities of American policies changing anything in East Asia are limited and that a far-sighted U.S. policy would "plan for a gradual and tactful disengagement from the Nationalist cause in Taiwan" and "abandon all restrictions on trade with and travel in China, *unilaterally and without reciprocity.*" (Italics added) Only by gradually inducing China to join the world community, he says, "will our children thank us for saving them from inheriting a world more bitterly divided than at any time in its history."

A month later, on March 20, Senator Edward M. Kennedy made an outstanding address in New York in which he deplored the folly of beginning an ABM system allegedly deployed against China, found no evidence that she was an expansionist power and submitted that considering the folly and futility of our efforts to isolate China "it is unrealistic to expect Peking to take the initiative" in renewing relations. He urged that we take seven steps in this direction, including attempts to reopen the Warsaw talks, unilaterally doing away with restrictions on travel and non-strategic trade, and offering to restore consular services and to discuss full diplomatic relations while withdrawing our opposition to Peking's entry into the United Nations. For twenty years, he said, "our China policy has been a war policy," one which must be reversed.[4]

Our need to work with the Soviet Union to dampen down dangerous conflicts in the Old World is now generally recognized. In a significant discussion of our responsibility for world order, Charles Yost says: "One's

[4] *Congressional Record*, March 24, 1969.

reluctant conclusion is that over the next decade the effective responsibility for international security may rest very largely with the United States and the U.S.S.R., either in competition or cooperation, or more likely in some untidy combination of the two." [5]

6. *Insist on domestic priorities.* This is the rule on which everything else depends. With our air and waters already dangerously poisoned, other natural resources being remorselessly ravaged, great numbers of rural people living in degradation with little hope, even for the young, many of whom starve slowly and die early; with our cities rapidly decaying, dooming great numbers of our people to the living death of hopeless ghetto life, and entire urban areas becoming unlivable even for the affluent—with our whole system so obviously failing before the world, we have no choice but to insist that our own house be put in order before we even consider imposing our way of life on many other peoples who have old and valid ways of living.

Scandalous and growing failure at home must doom any empire that we can build or seek to maintain abroad.

7. *Work to reduce our military and space budgets.* Ever since the start of World War II our national prosperity has been powered, or has been believed to be, by huge military-space expenditures, most of the end products of which are not socially useful. This has created enormous vested interests and military-industrial

[5] Charles W. Yost, "World Order and American Responsibility," *Foreign Affairs*, October 1968, pp. 1–14. The author was Deputy U.S. representative to the UN from 1961 to 1966.

partnerships which are on the point of becoming un-controllable.

Nothing in our entire national life is more urgent than this. Fortunately, too, in 1969 the public is disgusted and alarmed by the social scandal of interminable billions poured into Vietnam, year after year, with the returns flowing back in coffins and cripples. Fear and revulsion have been aroused also by the sudden realization that the Military-Industrial Complex is set to endanger most of our cities by building anti-missile bases near them, to be expanded indefinitely—first against a mythical Chinese peril (for 5 billions) and then against an alleged Russian threat (for 50 billions up). The "thick" ABM system would also involve a demand for an enormous system of underground shelters, to make "credible" our determination to slug it out with missiles —expecting to lose many millions of citizens but to "save" some by enabling them to emerge into a desolated radioactive world for a look around, before succumbing to the fallout, or, at best, to hunger and utter privation.

The concurrent demonstrations of the mortal perils and never-ending wastes involved in supporting the M-I complex should lead us to curb its destructive operations, while there is still time. This is the more urgent because the gigantic sums poured into it coffers are so desperately needed to save our national life from ever more dangerous decay at its foundations.

It must be firmly kept in mind that our military scientists can always propose more and more "scientific" and expensive "weapons systems," down to the very hour when one of them explodes or is exploded into the final doomsday—which must happen unless we use the most determined common sense to enforce a halt in this deadly progression.

Of course it is said that we must continue to practice "deterrence" until doomsday. One little slip behind and we are lost! But this is the perfect description of a mad policy, not a rational one. In a careful examination of Raymond Aron's theories of war, Benedict J. Kerkvliet, of the University of Wisconsin, recently found himself "unconvinced of the need for deterrence and an arms race; such strategy at times seems to be only a rational one for insane societies." [6]

This realization must spread rapidly among us, if we are to avoid the increasingly rapid destruction of our society internally under the guise of protecting it—or its sudden end through the use of the engines of deterrence. Their perpetual escalation must destroy us, one way or the other.

8. *Encourage genuine business partnerships with the weaker peoples.* There are unquestionably constructive aspects of our economic expansion abroad. New jobs, products and technology all help the foreigners affected, but these benefits can be shared without exclusive or overwhelming ownership by American companies. It does not help much, either, for a percentage of minority shares to be so widely distributed that no local voice in control is achieved. The best defense against nationalization and

[6] *International Studies Quarterly*, December 1968, pp. 439–40.

charges of monopoly is a genuine sharing with the peoples who provide the profits.

In late 1968, even the industrialized European states were finding defense against American economic control increasingly difficult. On November 24, C. L. Sulzberger wrote in *The New York Times* that "The enormous productive and management capacities of the United States exert a powerful and mounting pull on Europe's evolution."

9. *Give genuine, untrameled aid to the underdeveloped peoples through the United Nations and the World Bank.* One of the worst scandals of our relationship with the poor peoples is the forms of aid which the rich nations impose on them. Loans are freely available, at good interest rates. The money is spent but the interest continues. Then new loans are made, partly to pay the interest charges on the old ones, until the interest payments eat them up. Loans must usually be spent, also, for the purchase of American goods, even if better prices can be obtained elsewhere or much nearer home.

For arms sales to the poor peoples, interest-free loans are always available, with perhaps the last third of the price written off. This is called "aid." Since 1950 the United States has sold $37 billion worth of surplus arms and has $15 billion in outstanding orders. Credit from private Western firms at 10 per cent interest is also called aid. In the next twelve years India will need $14 billion in assistance just to service its debts and another $4 billion in new aid; and by 1975 the net benefit of all loans to the Less Developed Countries (LDCs) from the More Developed Countries (MDCs) will be near zero. These figures are taken from a startling study by Arnaud de Borchgrave, "Scandal of the Century," in *Newsweek*, October 30, 1967. He quotes George Woods, president of the World Bank, as seeing in the worsening imbalance between the LDCs and the MDCs "the gathering storm of a global economic crisis." Woods argues that all aid to the LDCs should be untied and multilateral or nothing. In other words, it should be administered by a world agency solely to help the LDCs, not mainly for the benefit of the rich northern nations, capitalist and communist. It is a measure of the callousness of the MDCs that the International Development Association, a World Bank Affiliate that tries to help the neediest of the needy, is broke.

10. *Accept a fair revision of the terms of trade between the LDCs and the MDCs.* A leading reason for the deepening gap between the rich Northern nations and the Southern poor ones is the ancient one of the industrialized lands dictating the prices they will pay for the primary products of the underdeveloped areas—cotton and coffee, meat and fruit, tin and rubber, copper and aluminum. The underdeveloped have to sell; the developed buy when they wish, on their own terms, and they also invent substitutes freely, such as synthetic rubber, which diminish or destroy the market for a primary product.

Inside their own rich countries the MDCs regulate prices to yield high prices and profits, even for agricultural products at times; outside they let the market take its course, destroy it or depress it. Thus the explosive gap between the developed and underdeveloped grows constantly wider and will continue to do so unless the MDCs will accept guaranteed prices for the primary products. But are we capable of this elemental justice? The United Nations Conference on Trade and Development—the North-South confrontation of the 122 LDCs with the handful of rich nations—has been laboring for three years, without persuading the developed nations "to take a single positive step" in the direction of its recommendations.

11. *Really use the United Nations to grapple with the world's crucial problems.* With the world population explosion gathering momentum all the time, the hopelessness of our attempting to repress social discontent and explosion everywhere would seem apparent, even if this were a moral undertaking. The revolution of rising expectations is a fact. Married to the technological revolution, it compels world-wide action to cope, even partially, with world-wide problems. The United Nations already has extensive machinery for doing this in its impressive social, labor, economic and cultural agencies.

Really putting our weight behind the United Nations and urging others to do so offers a fair chance of grappling with the world's most desperate problems. No other course does. World problems can be dealt with only by constructive world agencies.

12. *Make our own democracy work.* It can be strongly argued that this is the primary problem, for we cannot

help to establish workable agencies of world government —horrendous word—unless our own democracy functions at home. Otherwise we will continue to move toward some kind of fascism and the negation of all world cooperation. There is room for profound alarm also in the inability of our democratic processes to set us or keep us on a constructive world course. Especially depressing is the calamitous consequences of the great deception which President Johnson practiced in rejecting Goldwater's fiery foreign policy proposals and then promptly putting them into effect after the election of 1964.

Unavoidably, the validity of our democratic system now lives under a heavy cloud, both abroad and at home, and our 1968 electoral processes have not done much to lift it. But we must continue to strive to make our democracy work. We can still oppose every chauvinistic candidate, from local office to the highest, striving to make clear that our national purpose is peace and good neighborliness, including cooperative action to help our fellow men instead of suppressing them.

13. *Reorganize our national life and objectives for the long pull.* It is painfully clear that our national life has been subjected to wild gyrations during the past half century: from isolation into world war and collective security; back to isolationism, false prosperity and collapse; into world war and collective security again; on into globalism, *Pax Americana,* and world imperialism, promising rapid national decay and decline.

It is clear that the wildly swinging pendulum must be brought under control, but within what limits shall it be permitted to swing? Certainly not back into isolationism. We are a major part of mankind. We do have heavy responsibilities to work with other peoples, even to lead them in constructive directions. We do have the awesome responsibility of trying to help avert nuclear doom for humanity itself. We must try to help the peoples escape from suffocation by overpopulation and hunger. Retreating back into isolationism would even reduce our own living standards considerably. Nor can we continue to court national decline through our efforts to contain the Communist world and control the free one.

The dilemma of direction forces many leaders to search for a middle way, between isolationism and *Pax Americana*. This goal is natural and essentially right, yet we must not be misled by the word "middle." A long term plan for national living must not include semi-Vietnams and a commitment to helping the underprivileged peoples a little more with string-tied loans. It must not include a 50 per cent hostility to half the world.

What is required is a new sense of direction, a national decision to build here in the United States an enduring civilization. Of necessity the basis for a long term national life must be laid at home. We must come to a national decision to abolish the mortal danger of dying cities and huge rural slums, both of which exclude a large segment of our people from any meaningful living or the hope of it. Our productive apparatus is fabulous and it must now be turned largely away from dominating the world to rebuilding here at home the kind of life we say the lesser peoples must emulate. This means huge expenditures, perhaps mainly nongovernmental, but directed by government toward the goal of creating here a healthy, solidly based society. If this means also cleaning up our air and waters and greater attention to education and health, including many social services, this is the price we must pay both for long-term survival and for successful competition with the Communist societies. We believe our system is superior, and it is in some precious respects, but it is now incumbent upon us to demonstrate its survival values.

Unless we succeed here at home, we have no real role in the world. If we do succeed, many ways to cooperate with other peoples will open up. Then they will regard us with respect and admiration, instead of apprehension and hostility. Our leadership will be desired instead of shunned. Then we can help others to have a better life and to cope with the social perils that beset them.

This will mean that the real world community can grow, upon which the survival of human life on this planet depends. Which is it to be? Shall we lurch along fitfully into a short and painful future? Or shall we change course and build solidly for a long national life? For myself, I vote for revalidating the American Dream. I refuse to believe that we are destined to be a flash in the pan of the world's history, even a blinding one.

Index